MW01223250

America Online

FOR BUSY PEOPLE

Second Edition

Blueprints for America Online

On the following pages, we provide blueprints for some of the best ways to use AOL:

- Surf the World Wide Web

- Write an E-Mail Message

- Take Part in a Chat

- Check the Local Weather

- Check Out the Music Scene

- What's the Score?

- Take Stock of the Market

- Book an Airline Ticket

- Shop Till You Drop

Move forward or backward, go to your home page, or stop the action with the navigation buttons on the toolbar (pages 54-55).

Type in a Web address, starting with **www**, and then click Go to open the page in the browser (pages 55-57).

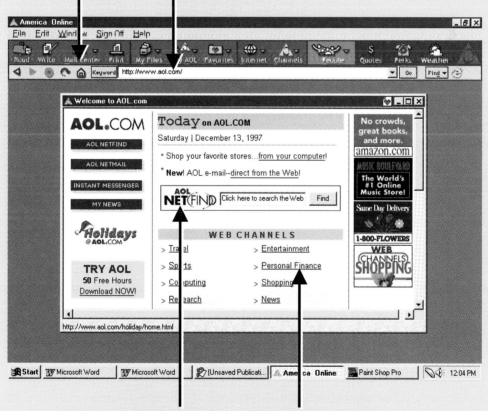

With AOL NetFind, you can easily locate people and places on the Internet (pages 58-59).

Click hypertext links to go directly to the referenced page on the Web (page 57).

Correspond with other AOL members, or with anyone who has an Internet address (page 76).

With the Send Later option, you can compose messages while you're offline and then send them with Automatic AOL (page 89).

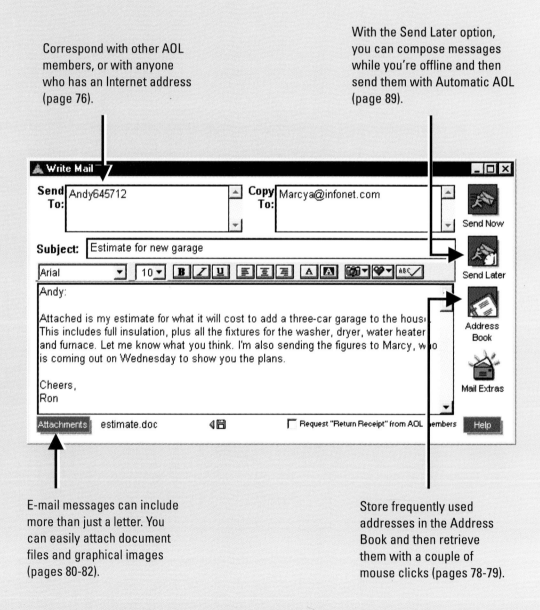

E-mail messages can include more than just a letter. You can easily attach document files and graphical images (pages 80-82).

Store frequently used addresses in the Address Book and then retrieve them with a couple of mouse clicks (pages 78-79).

Your comments as well as those of other participants appear onscreen just seconds after being sent (page 130).

See who's in the chat room with you and double-click a name to send that person an instant message (page 129).

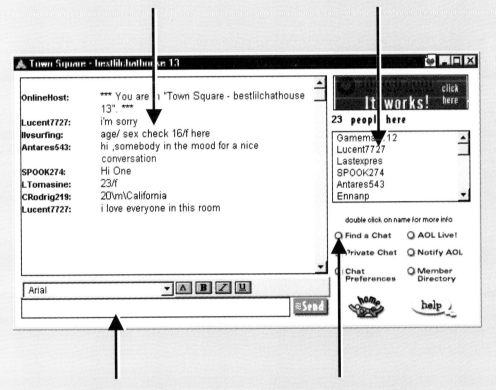

It's easy to take part. Just type in your thoughts here and then click send (pages 129-130).

With the Find a Chat feature, it's easy to locate a chat room on almost any topic, from romance to sports (pages 127-128).

Easily find out about the weather in any area of the country (page 171).

Who needs the TV weather person when you can get a complete forecast online? (page 170-171).

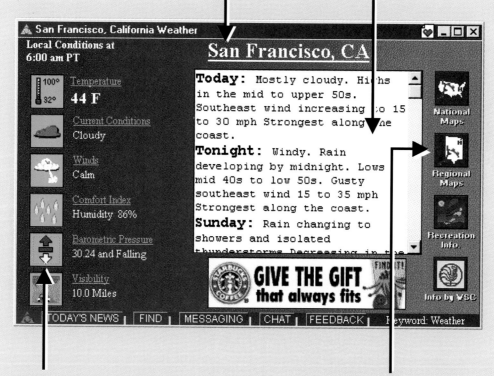

Want to know all about barometric pressure? Just click the button for a lesson in meteorology (page 171).

View weather maps and satellite photos to get the big picture on conditions where you live (pages 170-171).

Read reviews and even
download samples of the
latest popular CDs
(page 202).

Participate in online interviews
with top recording artists who
appear on AOL Live (pages 134-136).

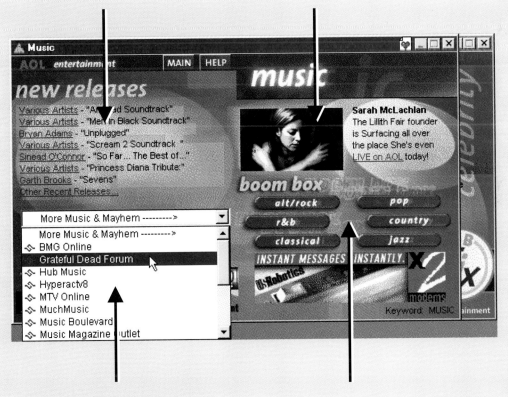

Choose from a long list of music
resources. There's even a forum
for you Deadheads out there
(page 203).

No matter what kind of music you like,
you'll find an area where you can get
information and share opinions with
other members (pages 126-129).

Scoreboards give you highlights of the day's action just moments after they happen (pages 206-207).

Need more than just the score? You can also get wrapups and box scores, or previews of games before they start, by clicking the letters to the left of the matchup (pages 207-208).

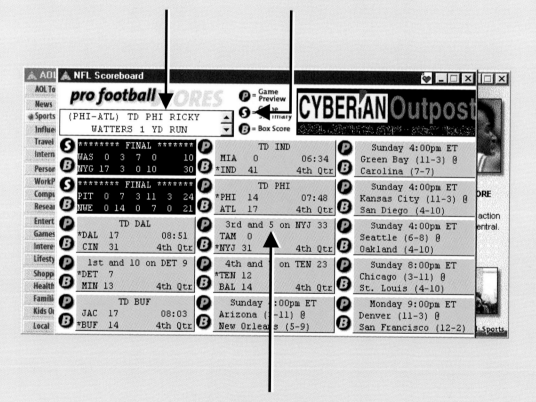

View all the latest results for your favorite sport, including up-to-date scores of games still in progress (pages 206-207).

Click one of these buttons to
display a window focusing on
a particular aspect of the market,
such as currencies (pages 218-219).

View a graph showing the
performance of the Dow Jones
Industrial Average or other
major index (pages 226-227).

Stay on top of the markets
with news summaries that
are updated throughout the
business day (pages 218-219, 223).

MarketDay gives you an overview
of the day's events, including
analysis of why key stocks moved
up or down (pages 218-219, 223).

With Preview Travel, you can be your own travel agent and find the flights that are best for you (pages 258-260).

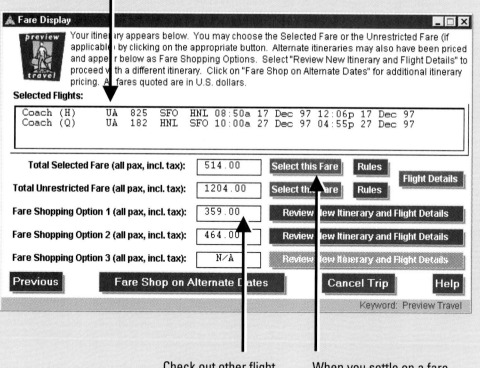

Fare Display

Your itinerary appears below. You may choose the Selected Fare or the Unrestricted Fare (if applicable) by clicking on the appropriate button. Alternate itineraries may also have been priced and appear below as Fare Shopping Options. Select "Review New Itinerary and Flight Details" to proceed with a different itinerary. Click on "Fare Shop on Alternate Dates" for additional itinerary pricing. All fares quoted are in U.S. dollars.

Selected Flights:

```
Coach  (H)      UA  825   SFO   HNL  08:50a  17  Dec  97  12:06p  17  Dec  97
Coach  (Q)      UA  182   HNL   SFO  10:00a  27  Dec  97  04:55p  27  Dec  97
```

Total Selected Fare (all pax, incl. tax): 514.00 [Select this Fare] [Rules] [Flight Details]

Total Unrestricted Fare (all pax, incl. tax): 1204.00 [Select this Fare] [Rules]

Fare Shopping Option 1 (all pax, incl. tax): 359.00 [Review New Itinerary and Flight Details]

Fare Shopping Option 2 (all pax, incl. tax): 464.00 [Review New Itinerary and Flight Details]

Fare Shopping Option 3 (all pax, incl. tax): N/A [Review New Itinerary and Flight Details]

[Previous] [Fare Shop on Alternate Dates] [Cancel Trip] [Help]

Keyword: Preview Travel

Check out other flight options that take you to the same destination but cost less (page 261).

When you settle on a fare, you can book your reservation and purchase the ticket, all online (page 259).

Look before you buy, thanks to full-color photos of merchandise ranging from chocolates to computers (pages 268-271).

You'll get a detailed description of each product, such as this "ultimate" Barbie doll from FOA Schwarz (page 271).

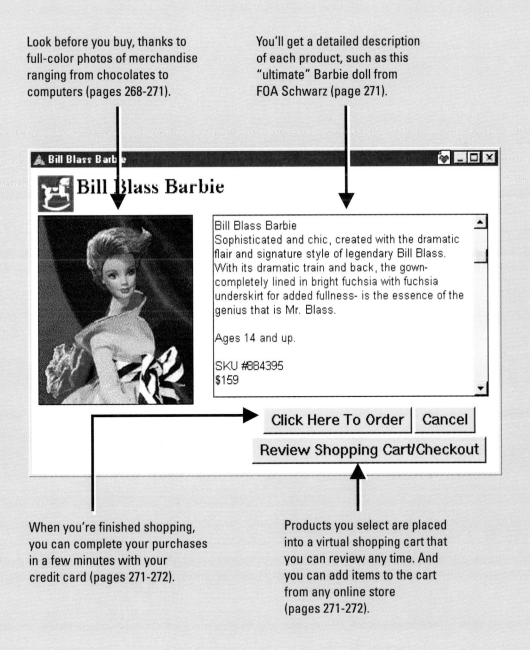

When you're finished shopping, you can complete your purchases in a few minutes with your credit card (pages 271-272).

Products you select are placed into a virtual shopping cart that you can review any time. And you can add items to the cart from any online store (pages 271-272).

America Online

FOR BUSY PEOPLE

Second Edition

The Book to Use When There's No Time to Lose!

David Einstein

OSBORNE

Osborne/**McGraw-Hill**

Berkeley / New York / St. Louis / San Francisco / Auckland / Bogotá
Hamburg / London / Madrid / Mexico City / Milan / Montreal / New Delhi
Panama City / Paris / São Paulo / Singapore / Sydney / Tokyo / Toronto

A Division of The **McGraw·Hill** *Companies*

Osborne/**McGraw-Hill**
2600 Tenth Street
Berkeley, California 94710
U.S.A.

For information on translations or book distributors outside the U.S.A., or to arrange bulk purchase discounts for sales promotions, premiums, or fundraisers, please contact Osborne/**McGraw-Hill** at the above address.

America Online for Busy People, Second Edition

Copyright © 1998 by The McGraw-Hill Companies. All rights reserved. Printed in the United States of America. Except as permitted under the Copyright Act of 1976, no part of this publication may be reproduced or distributed in any form or by any means, or stored in a database or retrieval system, without the prior written permission of the publisher, with the exception that the program listings may be entered, stored, and executed in a computer system, but they may not be reproduced for publication.

1234567890 DOC DOC 901987654321098

ISBN 0-07-882402-8

Publisher: Brandon Nordin
Editor-in-Chief: Scott Rogers
Acquisitions Editor: Joanne Cuthbertson
Project Editor: Nancy McLaughlin
Editorial Assistant: Stephane Thomas
Technical Editor: Jenn Thompson
Copy Editor: Judy Ziajka
Proofreader: Jeff Barash
Indexer: David Heiret
Computer Designers: Roberta Steele, Michelle Galicia
Series and Cover Designer: Ted Mader Associates
Series Illustrator: Daniel Barbeau

Information has been obtained by Osborne/**McGraw-Hill** from sources believed to be reliable. However, because of the possibility of human or mechanical error by our sources, Osborne/**McGraw-Hill**, or others, Osborne/**McGraw-Hill** does not guarantee the accuracy, adequacy, or completeness of any information and is not responsible for any errors or omissions or the results obtained from use of such information.

About the Author
David Einstein is a business and technology reporter for the *San Francisco Chronicle.* He is also the author of *PCs for Busy People* (Osborne/McGraw-Hill, 1996).

Contents at a glance

Contents

Part 2   AOL AND THE INTERNET

Part 3

MAKING THE MOST OF YOUR TIME ONLINE

INTRODUCTION

The online revolution is in full swing, and America Online is leading the charge. Thanks to explosive growth over the past several years, it is now the largest commercial online service by far, boasting more than 10 million subscribers and still growing. AOL has attained its leadership position thanks to a slick look and feel that make it easy to use, combined with rich content that offers something for everyone. There's news and information on hundreds of topics, as well as access to the Internet and electronic mail. But this plethora of possibilities can be confusing. The key to using AOL is knowing how to get the most out of it without getting lost in it.

That's where this book comes in. Like others in Osborne/McGraw-Hill's *Busy People* series, it's designed for people who don't have time to learn by trial and error, or by wading through technical jargon. This second edition of *America Online for Busy People* is an easy-to-read book for people who—to paraphrase Sergeant Friday of Dragnet fame—just want the facts.

I Know You're in a Hurry, So...

Let's get down to cases. To use AOL, you're going to need the right equipment. That means either a personal computer with Microsoft Windows or a Macintosh. AOL runs much the same on either system, but this book is directed at Windows users (hey, that's life; for every Mac in the world, there are nine PCs). In particular, I'll deal with AOL's new Version 4.0 software for Windows.

You'll also need a modem. That's the device that lets your PC communicate with another computer—which in this case will be the system at AOL headquarters in Virginia. Most PCs today come with internal modems, the latest of which are rated for speeds up to 56 kilobits per second. That's fast enough to let AOL's flashy graphics appear onscreen in just seconds.

America Online for Busy People is an indispensable book for anyone just getting started with AOL, yet it also contains plenty of goodies for PC users already familiar with the service. This book helps make it easy to:

- Customize your account
- Access the Internet and surf the Web
- Send and receive e-mail
- Chat with other AOL members
- Get inexpensive and free software
- Find out if the Giants won
- Track your stocks
- Further your education
- Shop online

As you can see, there's a lot of territory to cover, but don't worry. You don't have to be a computer genius to take advantage of what AOL has to offer. In fact, all you really have to know is how to turn on your PC. I'll teach you the rest.

Keeping Pace with the Future

Although services like AOL have experienced tremendous growth, they have found themselves threatened by another sort of online competition: the Internet. Once a government-backed network for scientists and professors, the Internet has blossomed into the greatest conduit of information the world has ever seen. And AOL has blossomed with it, integrating the Internet, and especially the graphically rich World Wide Web, directly into its service. Version 4.0 of AOL's software even provides a version of Microsoft's popular Internet Explorer Web browser, built right into the main window where you can always get at it. The Internet has become such an important part of being online that the entire second part of this book is devoted to it, with chapters discussing the Web, e-mail, and newsgroups.

Things You Might Want to Know About This Book

Because the whole purpose of the *Busy People* series is to help you work quickly and efficiently, this book is designed to give you answers to your questions, not fill your head with useless information. It's arranged so that if you want to know about a specific topic, you can go right to it, without having to plod through material that doesn't interest you. If you're new to AOL, it's probably best to start at the beginning and get the basics out of the way first. If you're already familiar with the service, but aren't yet up to speed on the Internet, the chapter on the World Wide Web would be a good starting point. In any event, feel free to hop around.

Throughout the book, you'll encounter a number of elements designed to help make your reading experience more enjoyable and informative. Here's a rundown of some of them:

Blueprints

The Blueprints at the front of the book demonstrate some of the interesting things you can do with AOL.

Fast Forwards

Each chapter begins with a Fast Forward section. These sections are just the thing for people who are impatient, or already experienced with AOL, or both. They describe major themes of the chapter in just a few words, and provide page references to more in-depth treatments of each topic within the chapter. Brief and handy, the Fast Forwards are all some readers will need for certain topics.

Expert Advice

This feature—accompanied by a picture of a man at a chessboard—suggests time-saving tips and techniques that can make your computing experience more efficient and productive. Think of Habits & Strategies as habit-forming notes that let you see the forest through the trees and help you plan ahead.

Shortcuts

If there's one thing busy people need, it's the ability to do things faster. When there's a way to do something that's not as conventional as the normal method described in the text, but is *faster*, I'll tell you about it. Just look for the man jumping over the fence with his tie flying in the breeze.

Cautions

Whenever you work on a PC, there's the possibility of making a mistake and spending time trying to discover what went wrong. In some instances, you can even mess up your computer system by flailing around. That's why we include this feature. The guy in the hard hat will warn you of possible pitfalls, and how to avoid them.

Definitions

I'll try my best to avoid computer technobabble, but when I must use it, I'll usually explain a term the first time it occurs in the text. If a more thorough definition is called for, you'll find it right next to a body builder (who's beefing up his technical vocabulary). That way, you can read the definition if you want to and refer back to it whenever necessary. (Or you can ignore it, which is probably what I'd do most of the time.)

Step by Step

To help clarify some of the more detailed AOL procedures, blue Step by Step boxes will walk you through the necessary stages, using helpful screenshots from AOL.

Let's Do It!

Okay, now that you've had your Busy People orientation course, it's time to get up and running with America Online. Because everybody knows that the place to be in the '90s is online, and the place to be online is AOL. So turn on your computer and let's get connected!

Part 1

The Basics for Busy People

Learning and Using AOL: Channel Surfing Made Easy

INCLUDES

- Exploring the AOL channels
- Moving around in AOL
- Menus and the toolbar
- Using keywords
- Finding stuff fast
- Favorite Places

FAST FORWARD

Display the Channels Window ➤ p. 7

When you sign on to AOL, the Channels window is hidden behind the Welcome window. To view the channels, do one of the following:

- Click the button labeled AOL Channels in the Welcome window.
- Close the Welcome window by clicking the small "x" in the upper right-hand corner.
- Use the keyword **channels**.

Use the Toolbar to Cut to the Chase ➤ pp. 15-16

The AOL toolbar provides quick access to AOL's key areas and features. The colorful buttons across the top of the main AOL window are always available as long as you're signed on. If you're not sure what a button does, just place your mouse cursor over it, and a descriptive label will pop up.

Use Keywords to Go Places Instantly ➤ pp. 15-16

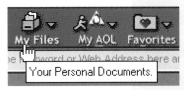

The Keyword feature allows you to specify a word or words that will quickly take you to a chosen area within AOL. Here are a few ways to use keywords:

- Enter a keyword in the space on the toolbar and then click Go.
- Click the Keyword button on the toolbar and then enter the word you want and click Go.
- Press CTRL-K, enter the word you want, and click Go.

Find Something Easily ➤ pp. 17-20

Locating people, places, and events among the thousands of features on AOL can be a challenge, but don't worry. You can find stuff in a jiffy using powerful search features. The place to start is Find Central, which you can access from the Find menu on the toolbar or by clicking Find in the Channels window.

Save Your Favorite Places ➤ pp. 20-22

Whenever you find an area on AOL—or on the Internet—that you
really like, save it in your Favorite Places folder so you can have easy
access to it in the future. Here are a couple of ways to do this:

- Click the little red heart in the upper-right corner of a window.
  Then click Add to Favorites in the dialog box that pops up.
- Drag the heart to the Favorites button on the toolbar.
- Click the Favorites button and choose Add Top Window to
  Favorite Places. Then click Add to Favorites.

Get Help When You Need It ➤ pp. 24-25

This book will teach you the basics of using AOL, but if you need
more help, you can get it easily. Here's how:

- If you're not signed on, choose Offline Help from the Help
  menu. This feature lets you search for assistance on basic topics,
  including problems with connecting to AOL.
- When you're signed on, choose Member Services Online Help
  from the Help menu. You'll be taken to the Member Services
  area, where you can get in-depth answers to your questions.
  You can even ask other members for their opinions.

America Online didn't get 10 million members by being difficult to use. In fact, its enormous popularity is largely due to the fact that it's extremely easy to use, even for beginners—and with the latest rendition of its Windows software, Version 4.0, it's even easier and more fun. In fact, with its splashy colors and flashy graphics, you might get the feeling that you're on the bridge of a starship, rather than sitting at your personal computer. In this first chapter, you'll discover how to navigate around the service like a pro while becoming familiar with some of the key features of this brave new online world. (If you're not already a member, go straight to Chapter 2 to find out how to become one.)

Signing On

When you first start AOL, you'll see the Sign On dialog box shown in Figure 1.1. It displays the last screen name that was used to access the account. To select another screen name (you can have up to five on your account), click the arrow to the right of the name. Then enter your password and click SIGN ON. The program will then go through several sign-on steps. It will:

1. Get your modem's attention.
2. Dial your primary access number.
3. Connect to AOL's computer system in Virginia.
4. Verify your screen name and password and start your online session.

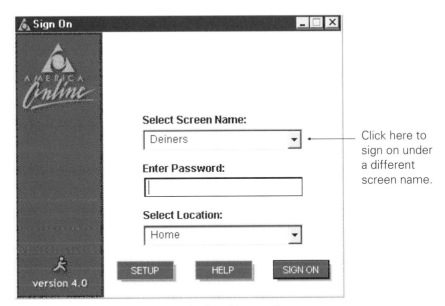

Figure 1.1 The Sign On window is the first thing you'll see.

When your PC and the AOL computer hook up, the speed of your connection will appear briefly on the screen. The speed can vary depending on several factors, including the quality of signal on your telephone line and the speed of your modem. Even with a 56 kbps modem, you'll probably never see speeds higher than about 48,000.

During sign-on, a three-panel display appears on the screen to keep you informed of how the process is going.

DEFINITION

Dialog box: A window (usually small) in which you are asked to make choices such as whether to open or save a file or change preferences—so, in a sense, you're having a dialog with your PC.

And Getting Off

Friends tell me that AOL can be mildly addictive. Nevertheless, there comes a time when every online session must end. To disconnect and quit the program, click the X in the upper-right corner of the main AOL window. To disconnect and return to the Sign On window (thereby keeping the program running), use the Sign Off menu on the toolbar. Why would you want to keep the program open after you have disconnected? One reason is so your PC can use Automatic AOL to sign on while you're away and check for things like new e-mail (see Chapter 4).

"Welcome!"

The same voice that welcomes you when you sign on will also tell you when you have mail and bid you good-bye when you sign off. He's nice, but some users find him a bit irritating after a time. In Chapter 2, I'll show you how to silence him.

In fact, that's exactly what you'll hear when you sign on to AOL with your multimedia PC: a friendly male voice ushers you in with a glowing "Welcome," and there, in front of you, is the Welcome window, shown in Figure 1.2. This is your online gateway, providing easy access to AOL's channels as well as to the People Connection (for live chats between members) and your mailbox. You can also get updates of the day's online activities on AOL Today, and you can get on the World Wide Web simply by clicking Go to the Web.

The Main AOL window

The Welcome window is inside a larger window. This is the main AOL window, which is always open while you're using the service. Across the top are the menu bar and toolbar, just as you'll find in most Windows programs. I'll talk

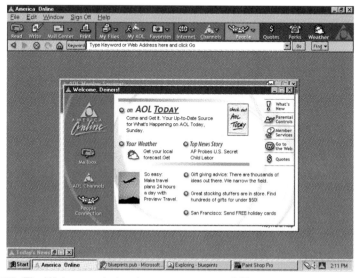

Figure 1.2 The Welcome window is your gateway to AOL.

about them a little later in this chapter. Right now, however, let's learn about the channels themselves.

The Channels Window

If the Welcome window is your gateway to AOL, your road map is the Channels window, shown in Figure 1.3. Here you'll find one-button access to the subject areas—called *channels*—into which the service is organized. When you sign on, the Channels window is there on your screen, but it's mostly hidden because the Welcome window is sitting on top of it. To view the Channels window, click the button labeled AOL Channels in the Welcome window. (From anywhere in AOL, you can display the Channels window by using the keyword **channels**.) Once in the Channels window, you can go to any channel simply by clicking it. You can also go to any particular channel by clicking Channels on the toolbar and choosing the channel you want from the drop-down menu. To return to the Welcome window from any place in AOL, use the keyword **welcome** (you'll learn about keywords in a minute).

Figure 1.3 The Channels window offers one-click access to any channel.

EXPERT ADVICE

This book isn't going to do you much good if you don't have Version 4.0 of the AOL software. If you're still using an earlier version, it's time to upgrade. You can do it easily by downloading the new software (and it's free). Just use the keyword upgrade *and follow the instructions.*

Unique Content, but a Common Look and Feel

Each channel focuses on a different broad subject: news, sports, entertainment, and so on. Yet all the channels share a common look and feel to make finding things easier. In most channels you'll find a listing of "departments," which are major content categories. Each channel also highlights features on timely topics. Most of the channels are covered in depth later in this book. In the meantime, here are descriptions of the channels.

AOL Today

This is your daily online guide to what's happening on AOL. It's updated throughout the day to help members stay informed and let them quickly locate featured programming. It's a good first stop whenever you sign on.

Computing

This channel has everything for the personal computer user. You can read top PC magazines and get technical support from hardware and software companies, and you can download useful software files from AOL's vast software libraries.

Entertainment

Capitalizing on the nation's fascination with television and movies, AOL has loaded this channel with news, features, and behind-the-scenes facts about Hollywood and your favorite TV shows. There's also plenty of stuff for you bookworms out there.

Families

On-the-go parents can get the most out of their valuable family time with practical information and advice on popular products and services, along with useful support groups.

Games

The PC has become a major platform for video games, and AOL is right there with shoot-em-ups, sports games, fantasy games, and role-playing adventures. On the Games channel you'll also find hundreds of games to download or play online, as well as hints and strategies for your favorite games.

Health

Want to lose weight? Get in shape? Eat better? Check out the latest trends and tips. You'll also have access to medical references and support groups providing information on illnesses and treatment suggestions.

Influence

Take an inside look at movers and shakers in the worlds of entertainment, art, and business. In addition to the latest gossip, you'll find timely information on fashion and upscale living.

Interests

This online community is your guide to real-life interests and hobbies, with resources on everything from pets to cars. If you want to improve your cooking or take better photographs, check it out.

International

AOL reaches across the globe. You can use this channel to find out what's happening in Canada, France, Germany, the United Kingdom, Japan, or just about any other country.

Kids Only

Want to wean your kids from television? Steer them to Kids Only, which specializes in entertainment and educational activities for children 6 to 12 years old. It's a safe, secure online environment for the younger set.

Lifestyles

Share ideas about religion, romance, self-improvement, gender, and other topics in this community-oriented channel. It's chock-full of forums that let you exchange opinions and learn about lifestyles other than your own.

Local

Your gateway to Digital City, which provides AOL members with local news and information about major cities across the country. It's perfect for keeping up with life where you live, for busy people who do a lot of traveling, and for the rest of us who just like to fantasize about being somewhere else.

News

Extra, extra, read all about it! This channel brings you breaking news plus in-depth coverage of the day's top stories in sports, entertainment, business, and politics.

Personal Finance

If you're talking money, you're talking the Personal Finance channel. You can do home banking, trade stocks online, and even manage your own mutual funds—plus you can conduct your own research on publicly traded companies. Who needs a broker, anyway?

Research & Learn

The public library is nice, but for real convenience you can't beat the 24-hour availability of AOL's collection of encyclopedias, dictionaries, almanacs, and other reference materials. And if you're a student, you can use this channel for interactive help with homework.

Shopping

Why bother to go to a mall when you can shop from the comfort of home? This channel offers a huge selection of products from more than 100 online stores featuring everything from chocolates to computers to casual clothes.

Sports

Forget the sports pages. With AOL, you can find out instantaneously who won, who lost, who got injured, and who got a rich new contract. Every major professional and college sport is covered, along with other sports such as pro wrestling, which newspapers tend to ignore

Travel

Whether you're looking for a bargain air fare to London or a good restaurant in Phoenix, this channel should be your first stop. It's loaded with resources that can make that next vacation or business trip more enjoyable—and less expensive.

Workplace

Here you'll find useful information and resources for finding a job, creating a new business, or expanding an existing one. Share your thoughts and ideas with other members in forums that focus on careers and the workplace.

Basic Techniques

If you're the least bit familiar with Microsoft Windows, you should have no trouble at all using AOL. The methods you'll use to manipulate files, move and copy text, and use the mouse on AOL are practically carbon copies of the methods used in most Windows-based programs. This section covers some of the basic techniques that will help you get things done quickly and easily.

Moving Between Windows

When you move from place to place in AOL, each new window you open is automatically placed atop the previous one. You can have an unlimited number of windows open at one time. To switch between open windows, click AOL's Window menu at the top of the screen and, from the list at the bottom of the menu, choose the name of the window you want to have displayed.

Closing and Minimizing Windows

Every window has three little boxes in its upper-right corner. To close a window, click the box farthest to the right—the one with the X in it. You can *minimize* a window by clicking the left box—the one with the single horizontal line. When you minimize a window, it shrinks to become a small bar near the bottom of the screen, like this:

Click here to restore the window.

To restore a window to its previous size, click the left box on the minimized bar. (Note: The middle box is for enlarging the window to fill the screen. Not all windows in AOL can be resized, but most can.

SHORTCUT

You don't have to manually close every window. You can close every window except the one on top by choosing Close All Except Front from the Window menu. And don't bother to close windows when you end your AOL session—they all close when you sign off.

The Hand That Points the Way

When you start playing with AOL, you'll find yourself jumping from place to place by clicking links to other areas. In Internet parlance, these links are called *hyperlinks*. When you move the mouse pointer over a hyperlink, the pointer turns into a hand with an extended forefinger, like this:

AOL is continually improving its software with new tools and features—but don't worry; you won't have to run out and get the new software. When new technology becomes available, AOL can download it to your computer while you're online.

Hyperlinks can be buttons, images, or text. On AOL, a single click on a hyperlink will take you to the area associated with the link—either on AOL or out on the Internet. (You'll learn about Internet hyperlinks in the next chapter.)

Menus Make Life Easier

The menu bar at the top of the main window contains five menus labeled File, Edit, Window, Sign Off, and Help. Clicking a menu opens a drop-down list of options, as shown here. These menus work just like most Windows 95 menus, but as you can see, they also include options that make it easier to use AOL. Throughout this book I'll point out ways to use the menus wisely.

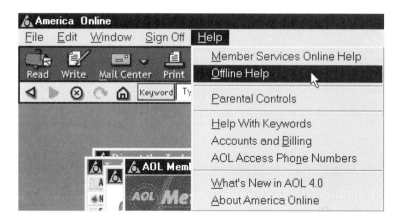

The Toolbar

The toolbar just below the menus consists of an upper row of buttons plus a lower row that includes the Find button and other tools for using keywords and the World Wide Web. (You'll learn how to use the Web in Chapter 3.) Several of the main buttons have downward-pointing arrows, indicating that they display drop-down menus when selected. Table 1.1 describes the key functions of the main toolbar buttons.

Keywords

The fastest way to get around in AOL is to use *keywords*. AOL's Keyword feature is the online version of the transporter in Star Trek, carrying you instantly from place to place. As the name implies, a keyword is a word—sometimes a pair of words, but usually just one—that transports you instantly to a specific area of the service. Often a keyword can save you several steps in the navigational process. There are thousands of keywords, with more being added all the time. To use a keyword, use either of the following procedures:

- Enter the keyword in the space on the toolbar and then click Go.
- Open the Keyword dialog box, shown in Figure 1.4, by clicking the Keyword button on the toolbar or by pressing CTRL-K. Then enter the keyword and click Go.

16

The last three buttons on the toolbar appear only if your monitor is set for at least 800-by-600 pixel resolution. To check the resolution or change it, click the Windows 95 Start button, choose Settings, and then choose Control Panel. On the Control Panel, double-click Display and then click the tab labeled Settings.

What if you forget what a tool does? Just place your mouse pointer over the tool for a moment. A brief description of the tool will appear in a yellow box.

Button	Name	Button Function
Read	Read	Opens your mailbox so you can read messages you've received and sent.
Write	Write	Opens a window in which you can compose a new message.
Mail Center	Mail Center	Opens a menu for reading, writing, and managing your mail.
Print	Print	Prints the text or picture that's displayed in the open window.
My Files	My Files	Opens a menu for accessing your Personal Filing Cabinet and reading mail offline.
My AOL	My AOL	Opens a menu for personalizing AOL to suit your tastes.
Favorites	Favorites	Opens a menu for viewing and managing Favorite Places.
Internet	Internet	Opens a menu for using the World Wide Web and Internet newsgroups.
Channels	Channels	Opens a menu of AOL's channels
People	People	Opens a menu for using chat rooms and sending instant messages.
Quotes	Quotes	Lets you quickly get the latest price for a publicly traded stock.
Perks	Perks	Tells you the advantages of being an AOL member.
Weather	Weather	Lets you get the current conditions and forecast for any place in the U.S.

Table 1.1 The AOL Toolbar Buttons

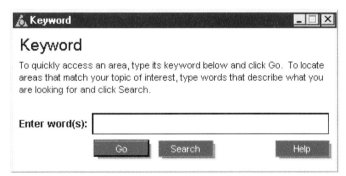

Figure 1.4 The Keyword dialog box

EXPERT ADVICE

If an area has a keyword, it will be shown at the bottom of the area's window. During your travels through AOL, be sure to note the keywords for places that you plan to visit again.

What If You Don't Know the Keyword?

Hey, don't panic. There are steps you can take if you don't know the keyword for an area.

- Enter a word or words in the Keyword dialog box that describe the topic you want and click Search instead of Go. A list of areas related to the topic will be displayed. You can then view descriptions of the areas and go directly to the areas.
- Use the keyword **keyword** to go directly to AOL's area for keywords, shown in Figure 1.5

Search and Ye Shall Find

America Online has a lot to offer—but if you can't find something, it may seem like it offers too much. Not to worry. Just use one of AOL's powerful searching tools. You can find them all in one place called Find Central. Find

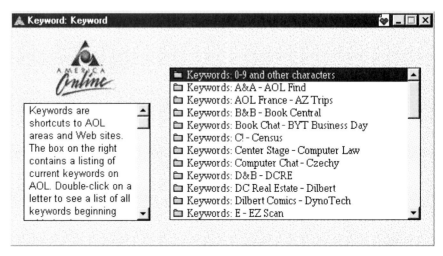

Figure 1.5 Find keywords using this alphabetical directory

Central is like having an online information booth at your service 24 hours a day. It lets you easily locate people, places, and events. To access Find Central, choose it from the Find menu on the toolbar or click Find in the main Channels window. Find Central offers a bunch of options, including:

- **Find It on AOL** Lets you search the entire service for topics that interest you.
- **Find It on the Web** Takes you to NetFind, a powerful engine for searching the World Wide Web (more on this in Chapter 3).
- **AOL Channel Guide** Gives you a quick rundown of the main features of any channel. As you can see in Figure 1.6, for instance, it lists all of the sports available in the Sports channel.

Finding Something Fast

Suppose you're a Star Trek fan (aren't we all?). To find content on AOL related to the show, go to Find Central and select Find It on AOL, or just click

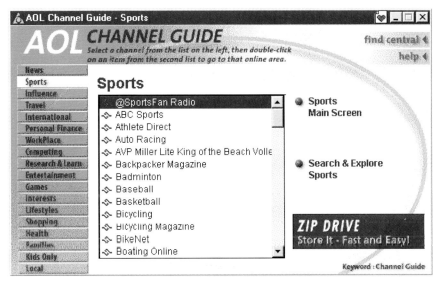

Figure 1.6 A quick guide to what's available on the channels

Find on the toolbar and choose Find It on AOL. Then follow the instructions in the step-by-step box on page 20.

SHORTCUT

The Channel Guide can actually cut down on the number of mouse clicks it takes to get to a given area. The easiest way to access the Channel Guide is to choose it from the Find menu, rather than first going to Find Central.

Easy Ways to Find People

Looking for another AOL member? If the person has created a Member Profile, you can find him or her through the Member Directory. To access the Member Directory window, shown in Figure 1.7, do one of following;

- Click People on the toolbar and then choose Search AOL Member Directory.
- Click Find on the toolbar and then choose AOL Members.

STEP BY STEP Finding Something on AOL

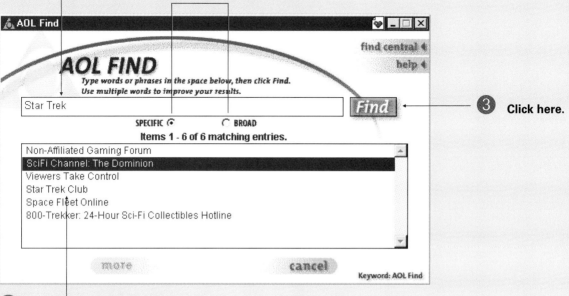

① Enter a description of what you're looking for.

② Indicate whether you want a broad or narrow search.

③ Click here.

④ Double-click a search result to get a description and go there.

You can search the Member Directory for the person's real name, screen name, location, or any other information in his or her Member Profile (see Chapter 2 for information on how to create one for yourself).

Favorite Places

Now that you've found what you want, wouldn't it be great if you could stash it away for quick and easy access in the future? You can, using AOL's Favorite

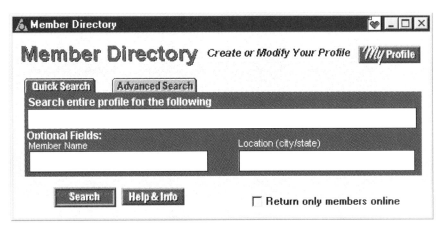

Figure 1.7 Use this window to find other members.

Places feature. Here's how it works: Almost every window in AOL boasts a red heart on its title bar. The heart indicates that the window can be saved as a Favorite Place. This can be done in several ways:

- Click the heart icon on the window's title bar and then click Add to Favorites in the dialog box that pops up.
- Drag the heart icon from the window to the Favorites button on the toolbar.
- Click the Favorites button, choose Add Top Window to Favorite Places, and then click Add to Favorites.

The Favorite Places feature can be used for almost any AOL window, World Wide Web window, or Internet newsgroup window. When you double-click a Favorite Place that's on the Web, AOL's Web browser starts and launches the site.

Managing Your Favorite Places

To view a list of your Favorite Places, click the Favorites button on the toolbar and then choose Favorite Places. This displays the contents of your Favorite Places folder. Turn the page to see what mine looks like:

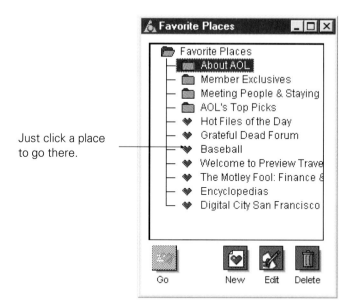

Just click a place to go there.

Favorite Places I've added appear with their heart icons at the bottom of the list. The folders at the top include areas that AOL automatically puts in your Favorite Places. To get rid of any item or folder, select it and click Delete. You can also add a new folder by doing the following:

1. Click New at the bottom of the Favorite Places window.
2. Check New Folder in the dialog box that appears.
3. Enter a name for the folder.
4. Click OK.

EXPERT ADVICE

You say you don't like the way your Favorite Places are arranged? So change them already! You can change the order in which places are listed by dragging them up or down or from one folder to another.

Your Personal Filing Cabinet

Speaking of keeping things in one place, as an AOL member you have a Personal Filing Cabinet in which AOL stores stuff that you accumulate during your time online. It holds and organizes items retrieved during Automatic AOL sessions (see Chapters 4 and 5), including e-mail messages and newsgroup articles. It also contains files that you've downloaded. And it can be used to permanently store copies of all the mail that you send and receive (Chapter 4 tells you how to do that). As you can see in Figure 1.8, the Personal Filing Cabinet has the same basic structure as Favorite Places.

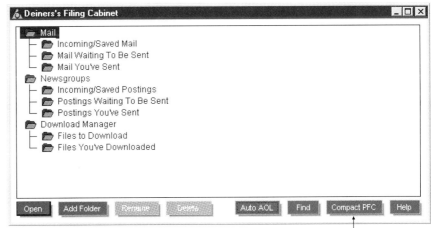

Click here to remove wasted space from your filing cabinet.

Each screen name for an account has its own Favorite Places and Personal Filing Cabinet. However, you can't use your Personal Filing Cabinet or Favorite Places when you sign onto AOL as a guest from someone else's computer.

Figure 1.8 AOL's Personal Filing Cabinet is easier to use than a regular filing cabinet.

Staying Organized

You can use buttons at the bottom of the Personal Filing Cabinet window to get rid of items you no longer want to keep or to rename any item. You can also use the Find button to hunt through the entire contents of the cabinet for specific text references, such as names in mail messages. Try *that* with a regular filing cabinet!

Getting Help!

After reading this book, you should be well-grounded in the basics. But if you need more help, you won't have far to look, because AOL has answers to almost any question you may have. When you installed the AOL software, a help file came as part of the package. Because it's always on your PC, you can use it to get answers to basic questions even when you're not connected. Just select the Help menu at the top of the screen and then click Offline Help. This will display a Help window that's similar to the Help windows in other Windows 95 programs. It lets you browse through an index or search for specific issues, such as problems connecting to AOL.

EXPERT ADVICE

If you're really stumped about some aspect of using AOL, you can get help from other members—and some of them are really experts. Just go the Member Services and click the icon for member help, or use the keyword members helping members.

Member Services

For help using AOL once you're online, the place to go is Member Services. To access this area, shown in Figure 1.9, choose Member Services Online Help from the Help menu, or use the keyword **member services**. The Member Services window includes a list of topics, and clicking any topic brings up a window with a list of subjects within the topic, letting you narrow your search for answers. There's also a button labeled Find It Now that you can click to quickly search for answers on any particular topic.

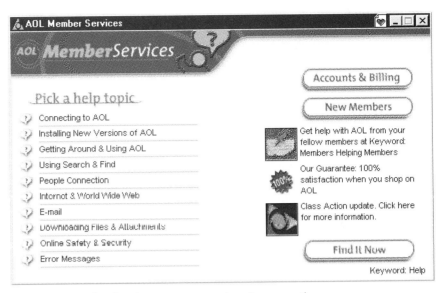

Figure 1.9 Member Services can answer almost any question.

EXPERT ADVICE

If you find yourself going to Member Services repeatedly with the same question, do yourself a favor and save the answer, or print it: with the text of the answer displayed, click Print on the toolbar.

CHECK POINT

I know you're eager to start roaming around AOL, but before we get to that, there are a few things you can do to make your online time easier and more productive. In Chapter 2, you'll learn how to personalize the world's biggest online service and make it your own.

2

Things to Do Once—and Other Stuff to Make Life Easier

INCLUDES

- Installing AOL's software
- Joining the AOL community
- Guarding your password
- Adding family members
- Protecting your kids
- Customizing your account

FAST FORWARD

Install the AOL software ➤ pp. 30-32

Welcome to America Online

In just a few minutes you'll be online! But first, we'll guide you through a short installation and registration process.

Please click inside the circle to let us know if you are:

○ Joining AOL as a new member
○ Upgrading to a new version of AOL
○ Adding your AOL account to this computer
○ Adding an additional copy of AOL to this computer

Click Next to continue.

You can't become an AOL member without the special software that lets you access and use the service. To get your free copy, call AOL at (800) 827-6364, or download the software from AOL's Internet site at http://www.aol.com. Installation is practically automatic—the software guides you through the whole process in just a few minutes.

Choose an Access Number ➤ pp. 32-34

AOL access phone numbers:

Area Code (707) - CA		
Santa Rosa	X2	523-1782
Santa Rosa	14.4	523-1048
Eureka	14.4	444-3091
Fairfield	14.4	426-3860
Napa	14.4	257-0217
Santa Rosa	K56	536-1691

As part of the process of starting an account, you'll be asked to choose telephone numbers that your PC will use to connect to AOL. You'll be presented with a list of numbers in your area. Look for numbers that are close to you and that support the fastest rate at which your modem can operate.

Change Your Password ➤ pp. 38-39

Old password:

Enter new password twice:

The only way to make sure that no one ever has unauthorized access to your account is to keep your password to yourself. Changing your password occasionally is an extra bit of insurance. To change your password:

1. Click My AOL on the toolbar and then choose Password, or just use the keyword **password**.
2. Enter your current password in the upper box and enter your new one twice in the lower boxes. Typing your password twice confirms the spelling
3. Click Change Password to make the new password effective.

Add Family Members to Your Account ➤ pp. 40-41

Create or Delete Screen Names

Screen Names
- About Screen Names
- IMPORTANT- Screen Name Policy
- How To Create and Manage Screen Names
- Create a Screen Name
- Delete a Screen Name
- Restore a Screen Name
- Update Screen Names on My Computer
- Parental Controls

Keyword: Names

Each AOL account can have up to five screen names, and each screen name can have its own e-mail, Personal Filing Cabinet, and Favorite Places—which means other people in your family can, in effect, have their own personal AOL accounts at no extra expense (but only one screen name at a time can be signed on). To create a new screen name, do this:

1. Click My AOL on the toolbar and then choose Screen Names.
2. Double-click Create a Screen Name.
3. Enter a new name in the box. Be creative, because with 10 million members, AOL long ago ran out of conventional names.
4. Click Create a Screen Name to complete the operation.

Give Yourself a Member Profile ➤ pp. 41-42

To let other members know about you—who you are, where you live, what hobbies you have, and other stuff—create a Member Profile for yourself. Here's how:

1. Click My AOL on the toolbar and then choose My Member Profile.
2. Fill in as many blanks as you like on the personal information form.
3. Click Update to store the profile in AOL's Member Directory.

Use AOL on Someone Else's Computer ➤ pp. 42-43

You can sign onto AOL from any computer that has the AOL software installed. Just do the following:

1. In the Sign On window, choose Guest from the drop-down list under Select Screen Name.
2. Click SIGN ON.
3. After the connection is made, you'll be asked to enter your screen name and password. Type them and click OK to complete the sign-on process.

Protect Your Kids with Parental Controls ➤ pp. 43-44

Although AOL is a family-style service, some areas, such as chat rooms and message boards, can go beyond what you might call G-rated material. And once you go out on the Internet, things can get way out of control. Fortunately, AOL provides Parental Controls that can help you limit your children's access to online sex, violence, and nasty language. To explore and use this feature, choose Parental Controls from the My AOL toolbar menu, or just use the keyword **parental controls**.

Being a busy person, you probably don't have a lot of time to spend installing software and setting it up. Don't worry, because AOL is so user friendly that you can start an account and be online in a matter of minutes. In this chapter, I'll guide you through the process of becoming a member. After that, I'll show you how to customize your account to make the AOL experience even more convenient and enjoyable for you and other members of your family. The whole thing is painless. Really. Trust me.

Installation and Setup

To use AOL, you need special software. To get the most out of the service, you need the latest version—4.0 for Windows 95. If you're already an AOL member but you're not yet using Version 4.0, you can download it from AOL. Just use the keyword: **upgrade**. If you aren't an AOL member, here are a couple of ways to get the latest software for free:

Many personal computers come with AOL preinstalled, so before you go looking for an AOL CD-ROM, make sure the software isn't already on your PC. If it is, skip the following section and go right to the part about setting up an account.

- Call AOL at (800) 827-6364. AOL will send you a CD-ROM containing Version 4.0.
- If you have access to the Internet, you can download the software from AOL's World Wide Web site at http://www.aol.com.
- AOL distributes millions of copies of its software in the mail, as well as packaging it with leading computer magazines.

Let the Software Be Your Guide

Getting started with AOL is a snap, because the software guides you through the process. Installation takes just a couple of minutes, during which the files in the program are copied into folders on your hard disk. Once that's finished, you'll be led through a series of prompts as the software sets itself up to work with your computer. It starts by searching for your modem—the device that lets the PC connect to AOL through the telephone line. In most instances, the modem is inside the computer, although you also can buy one that plugs into the back.

Info about Your Modem

To work with your computer, AOL needs to know a few things about your modem:

- What company made it
- The maximum speed at which it can send and receive data
- What COM port it's using

AOL will search your system for this information and then display a window like the one shown in Figure 2.1, showing you what it found. As you can see, I'm

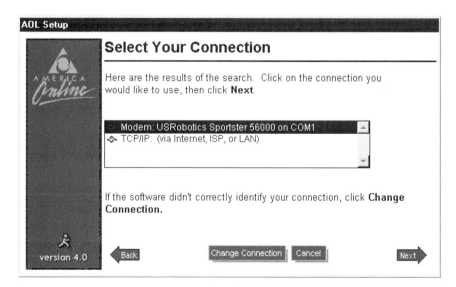

Figure 2.1 AOL automatically finds out what kind of modem you have.

using a U.S. Robotics modem running at 56,000 bits per second (56 kbps) on COM 1. If perchance the software doesn't correctly identify your modem, click Change Connection and set it straight.

DEFINITIONS

COM port: Communications port. Your modem uses a COM port to communicate with the PC. Most PCs have four COM ports, and most modems come preconfigured to work on COM 2. When AOL finds your modem during the installation procedure, it's best not to mess with the setting.

kbps: Kilobits per second. This is a standard way of measuring the speed of data transmission. A kilobit is 1,000 bits. A bit is the basic unit of digital information. The fastest modems for PCs are rated at 56 kpbs.

The Faster the Better Most PCs sold today come with modems capable of processing data at 33.6 or 56 kbps. The higher the number, the faster the modem, and the more efficiently you'll be able to use AOL. That's because AOL is a graphically rich service, and graphics take time to send over phone lines. If you have an older PC with a slower modem, you'd be well advised to buy a new one.

EXPERT ADVICE

Any time you want to check what kind of modem you have, do this: Click the Windows 95 Start button, select Control Panel, and double-click the Modems icon. Then click Properties to see the details about your modem.

AOL's Got Your Number

Okay, now you're ready to go through the process of joining the AOL community. Don't worry; it's painless (except for the normal pain associated with giving someone your credit card number).

The first step in the setup process is to find local telephone numbers you can use to connect to AOL's computer in Virginia. All you have to do is enter your area code. The software takes care of the rest, dialing a toll-free number and fetching a list of access numbers, which will be displayed in the window shown in Figure 2.2. Choose two numbers: one as a primary number and the other as a backup in case the first one is busy. Make sure the numbers support the fastest speed at which your modem can run.

Select a number and then click ADD to place it here.

AOL Setup

Select AOL Access Phone Numbers

- Select at least two AOL access phone numbers that will be used to connect your computer to the AOL service. To select a number, click on it then click **Add**.
- Select numbers that match or exceed your modem's speed (e.g., 28.8).
- When you're finished selecting numbers, click **Sign On**.

AOL access phone numbers:

Area Code (707) - CA
- Santa Rosa   X2   523-1782
- Santa Rosa   14.4 523-1048
- Eureka   14.4 444-3091
- Fairfield   14.4 426-3860
- Napa   14.4 257-0217
- Santa Rosa   K56 536-1691

ADD

Selected Numbers

More Info

Delete

Back   Cancel   Help   Sign On

Figure 2.2 Use this dialog box to set up your access numbers.

CAUTION

AOL tries to find access numbers that will be local calls for you. In some cases, however, a number may be outside your local area, in which case you'll pay toll charges every time you use it. That can be costly, so do yourself a favor and check with the phone company to make sure the numbers you pick are local.

SHORTCUT

Once you become an AOL member, you can find the latest AOL access numbers for any place in the world just by using the keyword access.

Changing Your Setup

When you created your AOL account, the setup information was stored in a location called Home. Over time, you might get a new PC, upgrade your modem, or move to another city. Or AOL might upgrade its access in your area with a new high-speed number. Don't worry; there's an easy way to deal with such changes:

1. Click SETUP in the AOL Sign On window to bring up the Connection Setup window.
2. To change an existing connection, select it and click Edit. This will display the AOL Setup dialog box shown in Figure 2.3, in which you can make your changes.
3. Click OK when you're done.

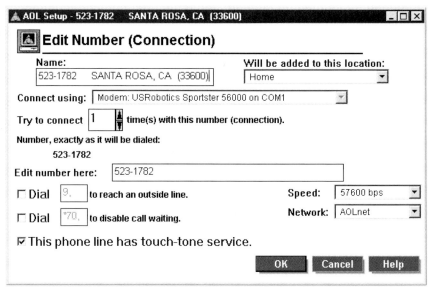

Figure 2.3 You can easily make changes to your connection setup.

To add a new modem, click the Connections tab in the Connection Setup window and follow the instructions. The Connection Setup window also contains a button labeled Add Location. This is especially useful for busy people who have AOL on their notebook computers. It lets you create separate locations for use at home, at work, or out of town in cities you frequent.

EXPERT ADVICE

Call waiting can cause problems in an online session. If you're connected to AOL and got a call, call waiting will break your online connection. You can disable call waiting for the duration of your AOL session by using the AOL Setup box shown in Figure 2.3..

Creating Your Account

After you choose your access numbers, AOL will disconnect you and then dial your new primary access number (thus saving themselves money—from now on, it's your dime, not theirs). Once you're reconnected, you'll be able to create your account online. The first thing you'll be asked for is the registration number and password you were given with your free software, which you enter in the window shown in Figure 2.4. This information allows you to get a free trial membership, which I'll talk about in a minute.

If you're already an AOL member and are reinstalling or updating to a new version of the software, click the appropriate box on the Welcome to AOL screen and enter your AOL screen name and password. This configures the software so you can use your account.

An Offer That's Hard to Refuse

Now it's on to the electronic paperwork—but it'll only take a minute or two. You'll be asked to provide your name, address, and day and evening phone numbers. Following that, you'll have to enter your credit card information so AOL can bill you each month. New AOL members start out with 50 free hours online to try out the service, plus the first month's fee is waived. That's what you call an offer you can't refuse. When the free trial period is over, you'll have the choice of several payment plans:

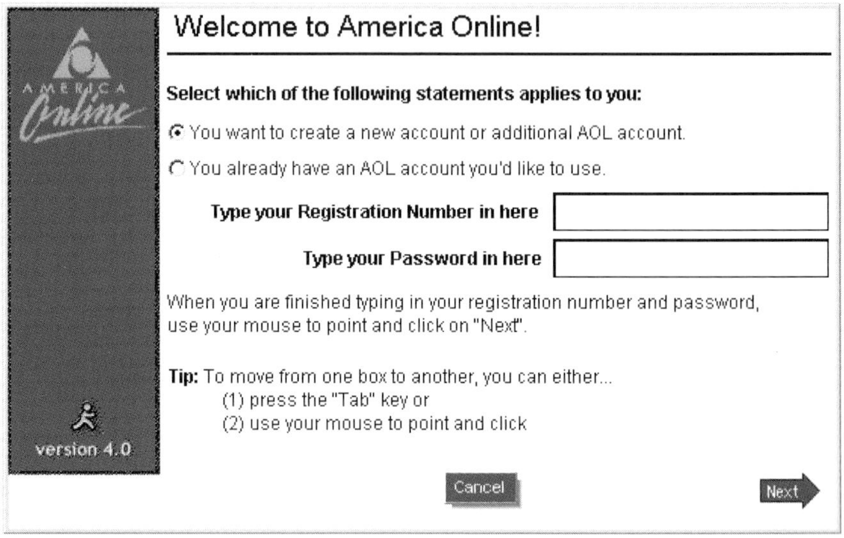

Figure 2.4 You'll need your registration number and password.

- **Standard Unlimited Plan** For $19.95 per month, you get unlimited access to AOL and the Internet with no hourly fees. This is the default plan, which you'll get unless you pick another one.
- **One Year Plan** Pay $215.40 up front, and you get a year's worth of service, which works out to $17.95 a month.
- **Bring Your Own Access (BYOA) Plan** If you already have an Internet connection, you can pay $9.95 a month to get unlimited access to thousands of AOL features.
- **Light Usage Plan** This is the way to go if you don't plan to spend much time online. For $4.95 per month you get three hours of AOL, including the Internet. Additional time is $2.50 per hour.
- **Limited Plan** This plan gives you five hours online for $9.95 per month, with additional time priced at $2.95 per hour.

Choosing an Identity

Before you can start using AOL, you have to pick an online name for yourself. Every AOL member has a unique *screen name* three to ten characters long

CAUTION

Pricing plans do not include premium services, such as some video games and reference features, which carry additional charges. For more information, go to the Premium Services area by using the keyword **premium services.**

that identifies him or her. But if you're thinking of using your own first or last name, forget it. Unless you have a very unusual name, it's probably already been taken by one of AOL's other members. It's the same sort of situation that you run up against when you're looking for a name to put on a vanity license plate. Go ahead and try your first name, your last name, or even your dog's name. If they're already spoken for, AOL will suggest a name that nobody else has, trying to get as much of your own name into it as possible. Figure 2.5 shows the unfortunate name it came up with for me after I tried *Einstein* and then *DEinstein*:

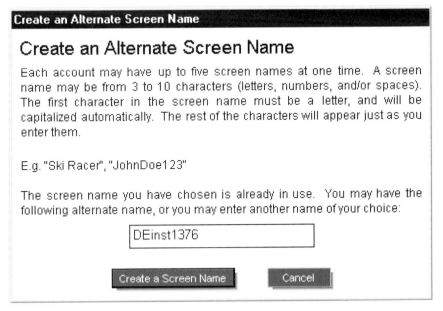

Figure 2.5 With 10 million members, good names are hard to find!

CAUTION

Be aware that once you pick a primary screen name for your account, you're stuck with it. Also, your screen name is your AOL e-mail address—another reason to choose an intelligible name if possible.

Picking a Password

The last step in establishing your new AOL account is choosing a personal password. This is a whole lot easier than coming up with a screen name, because AOL doesn't care if more than one member has the same password. Your password must be between four and eight characters long, and it can include letters and numbers. The password won't appear on the screen when you type—it will come out as a string of asterisks. You'll be asked to enter the password twice, just to make sure you typed what you meant to type.

EXPERT ADVICE

If you're the forgetful type, write down your screen name and password and put them in a safe place. Never give your password to a stranger. That's like an open invitation to run up charges on your account.

That's It—You're Ready to Go!

Congratulations. You're now part of the AOL community, and you can enjoy your new account 24 hours a day, 365 days a year. There's really nothing more that you have to do except sign on. However, there are a few things you can do to personalize your account.

Password Protection

The best way to prevent unauthorized access to your account is to keep your password from falling into the wrong hands. (This is especially a threat if you have any KGB agents in your office.) Seriously, though, it's not a bad idea to change your password every once in a while. As they say, "It couldn't hurt." And it's easy to do:

1. Click My AOL on the toolbar and then choose Passwords, or just use the keyword **password**. Then click Change Password to display the dialog box shown in Figure 2.6.
2. Enter your current password and then enter your new one twice. To protect your privacy, the passwords appear as a string of asterisks, so typing the new one twice confirms that you spelled it the way you intended.
3. Click Change Password to make the change effective.

Storing Your Password

One of the simplest things you can do to streamline your AOL experience is to store your password. That way you won't have to enter it each time you sign on. To store a password, use the following steps:

1. Click the My AOL button on the toolbar and then click Preferences.
2. Click Passwords to display the Store Passwords dialog box.
3. Enter the password for your screen name and then check the Sign-On box.
4. Click OK.

When you enter a password, it appears as a string of asterisks.

Figure 2.6 Change your password using this dialog box.

CAUTION

Storing a password can be risky. Anyone can sign onto an account that has a stored password. The rule of thumb is that you should never store a password for an account on a computer that a stranger might have access to.

Multiple Screen Names

You can have up to five screen names on your account—four in addition to the primary name, which can't be deleted. What would you do with four extra names? Well, if you're wanted in several states, you could use them as aliases—but that's not what AOL had in mind. A better use would be to give them to other family members. Or you could use two of them yourself: one for business and the other for personal stuff. Each screen name requires its own password and gives the user his or her own e-mail, Personal Filing Cabinet, and if desired, Member Profile. (We'll get to Member Profiles in a minute.)

Creating a Screen Name

Use the following steps to create a new screen name:

1. Click My AOL on the toolbar and then choose Screen Names, or just use the keyword **names**. Either way, you'll see this window:

Having extra screen names is like giving everyone in the family his or her own personal AOL account. There's a catch, however. Only one screen name at a time can be signed onto AOL.

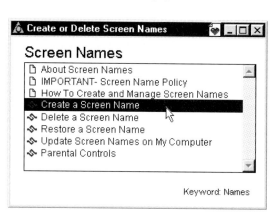

2. Double-click Create a Screen Name.

3. Follow the same steps you used in picking your primary screen name when you became an AOL member.

Getting Rid of a Screen Name

You can delete any screen name except the one with which you began your account. Just choose Delete a Screen Name from the window we just saw, and follow the instructions. When you delete a screen name, no one else can use if for six months. If, during that time, you decide you want the name back, click Restore a Screen Name in the same window.

EXPERT ADVICE

Don't like your original screen name? Just add another one and use it as your primary AOL identity. You'll be like Bernard Schwartz, who changed his name to Tony Curtis.

Changing Screen Names on the Fly

You don't have to sign off to let another family member use the account under his or her screen name. Instead, simply choose Switch Screen Name from the Sign Off menu. You'll see a list of all your screen names. Select the one you want and click Switch. This is also an easy way for you to switch to a different screen name in midsession.

Setting Up a Member Profile

The online experience can be pretty anonymous, with people identifying each other only by cryptic screen names. But you can let other AOL members know more about you by creating a Member Profile, which can include such information as where you live, your occupation, your hobbies, and even a personal quote that sums up your personality. Member Profiles aren't mandatory, but they take only a few minutes to create, and they can really help you get into the AOL community spirit. To create a profile, follow the step-by-step instructions shown on the next page.

STEP BY STEP Creating a Member Profile

1 Click My AOL on the toolbar and choose
My Member Profile to display this window.

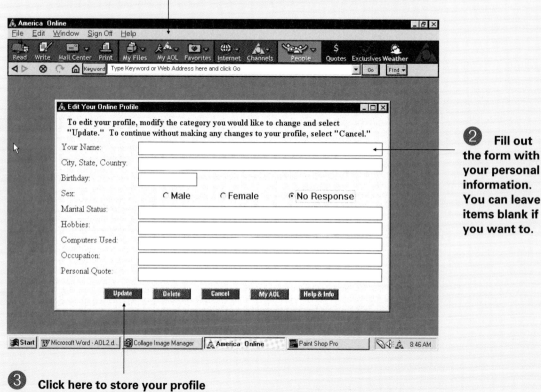

2 Fill out
the form with
your personal
information.
You can leave
items blank if
you want to.

3 Click here to store your profile
in the AOL Member Directory.

Signing On from Someone Else's Computer

One of the most convenient features of AOL is the ability to sign on from
any PC that has AOL installed on it. Say you're visiting a friend, and you want to
check your e-mail. Here's what you do:

1. Start AOL and choose Guest from the drop-down list of screen names.
2. Click SIGN ON.

3. When the connection is made, you'll be prompted to enter your screen name and password.

Once you've signed on this way, the time you spend online will be charged to your AOL account. Your friend will have to pick up any telephone surcharges—but hey, that's what friends are for.

Keeping Your Children Safe

Although most of AOL's content falls under the "G" rating category, there are certain areas in which the subject matter drifts into territory more suited to adults than children. In addition, AOL has no control over what you see when you venture out onto the Internet. That's where Parental Controls come in handy. This feature, shown in Figure 2.7, lets you limit your kids' access to online material. Specific ways to use these controls will be discussed at appropriate points in this book. At any time, however, you can invoke, disable, or change Parental Controls. Just choose Parental Controls from the My AOL menu on the toolbar or use the keyword **parental controls**.

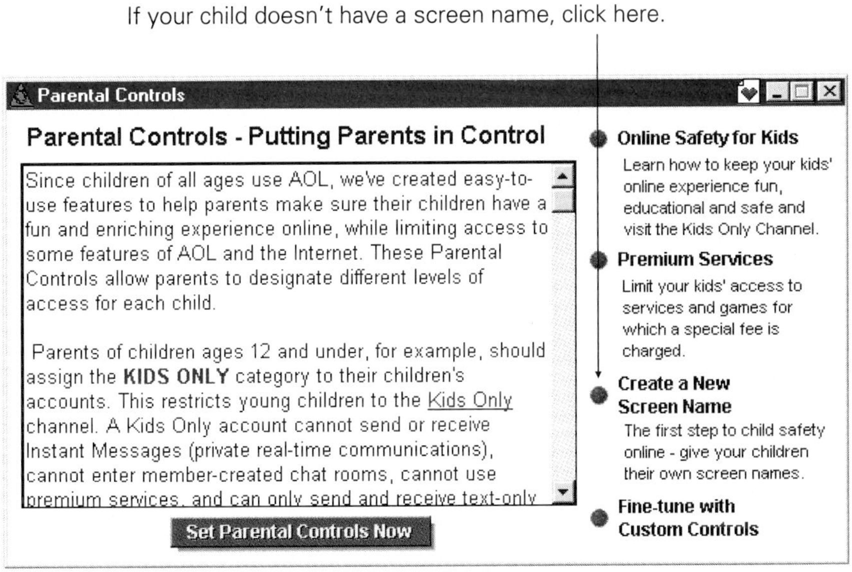

If your child doesn't have a screen name, click here.

Figure 2.7 Use Parental Controls to ensure a safe online experience for children.

EXPERT ADVICE

To use Parental Controls you have to be signed on under the primary screen name for your account. That means if your kids know your password, they can change the controls. So do yourself a favor and keep the password a secret between you and your spouse.

A Few Customizing Tips

Just because you're now part of a community of 10 million people doesn't mean you forfeit your individuality. AOL allows you to tailor various parts of the service to suit your needs. You already learned how to change and store your password. In future chapters, I'll show you how to customize aspects of e-mail, chat rooms, and the World Wide Web. Right now, let's take a look at some of the things you can do to adjust the general way in which AOL works for you.

Shut Up, Already!

AOL is a multimedia experience, which means that it offers sounds as well as colorful graphics. For instance, when you sign on, a voice says "Welcome," and when you quit, a voice says "Good-bye." Okay, so that's not very thrilling, but in other cases, this feature can be quite useful. When you have new e-mail, for instance, the voice tells you so. In some situations, however, you may not want to hear voices coming out of your computer. For instance, you may be using AOL at your office, and co-workers might not appreciate the noise. Fortunately, you can turn off the sounds. Here's how:

1. Choose Preferences from the My AOL menu on the toolbar and then click General to display the dialog box shown in Figure 2.8.
2. Deselect the box labeled Enable Event Sounds by clicking it.
3. Click OK to save the new setting.

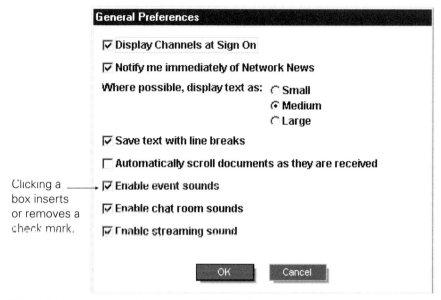

Clicking a box inserts or removes a check mark.

Figure 2.8 Set general preferences using this dialog box.

Tailoring the Toolbar

The AOL menus and toolbars together take up about 1 inch of the top of your computer screen. You can reduce that a little and claim some more screen real estate by changing the main toolbar so that it shows just names rather than names and pictures. Here's how:

1. Choose Preferences from the My AOL menu.
2. Click Toolbar.
3. Under Appearance, click Text Only. Then click OK. The toolbar should now look like this:

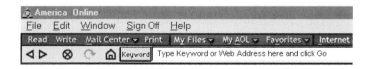

There's also an option to move the toolbar to the bottom of the screen, although why anyone would want to do that is unclear.

Make Things Easier on Your Eyes

If you find the text in your AOL windows hard to read, you can enlarge it. Go to General Preferences the same way you did in the preceding section. Then, under "Where Possible, Display Text as," choose Large instead of Medium. (Medium is the default size for text.) This will increase the size of type in text windows throughout AOL. It will also give you larger type for chat sessions and message groups. Figure 2-9 shows examples of medium and large type.

Offers You Can Refuse

Like many big organizations with lots of members, AOL makes its mailing list available to other companies, which could translate into an increase in the

NEW YORK (Nov. 22) - Hopes for peace in the troubled Korean peninsula re-emerged after a major breakthrough in preliminary talks aimed at reducing tension in the world's last Cold War flash point.

"Medium" is the default size for text.

NEW YORK (Nov. 22) - Hopes for peace in the troubled Korean peninsula re-emerged after a major breakthrough in preliminary talks aimed at reducing tension in the world's last Cold War flash point.

"Large" text is easier on the eyes, but there's less of it onscreen.

Figure 2.9 You can enlarge your onscreen text for easier reading.

You can also use Marketing Preferences to tell AOL not to telephone or e-mail you with unsolicited offers. Unfortunately, this option doesn't apply to third parties, who can call you up any time day or night.

amount of junk mail stuffing your real-life mailbox at home. If you'd rather not receive unsolicited mail from AOL or its commercial partners, AOL understands and will accommodate you. Just do the following:

1. Choose Marketing in the Preferences window and then double-click Tell Us What Your Mailing Preferences Are.
2. Place an X in the boxes for the categories that you're interested in. If you don't want to get any mailings from AOL and/or outside companies, enter X's in the appropriate boxes at the right.
3. Click Send to transmit the form to AOL.

You can't say "online" anymore without also saying "Internet" in the same breath. The folks at AOL have been rushing to incorporate the World Wide Web and other Internet features into their service, so let's rush with them. Next stop: cyberspace and the Web!

Part 2

AOL and the Internet

Gateway to the World Wide Web

FAST FORWARD

Get Yourself on the Web ➤ pp. 53-54

Getting onto the World Wide Web with AOL is easy. Here are a few ways to do it:

- Click Go to the Web in the Welcome window. This will take you to AOL's own home page on the Web.
- Choose Go to the Web from the Internet menu in the main window or click the Home icon on the toolbar (the little house). This will take you to your browser's home page.
- If you know the Web address you want, enter it in the address space on the toolbar and then click Go or press ENTER.

Use Hyperlinks to Navigate the Web ➤ p. 57

Technology News
(Nov 14 12:09PM)
- AOL Expands High Speed Access
- U.S., Europe At Odds On Satellites
- Lost Order Hammers Profits
- IBM Begins Restructuring
- Ellison Says Apple Search Narrows

Moving around on the Web is easy, especially with hyperlinks. Just click any underlined text or linked graphic—you'll be transported elsewhere within a Web site or to another site, perhaps halfway around the world. And don't worry about getting lost. Just click the Back button on the browser's toolbar to return to the previous page or click the Home button to go back to the browser's home page.

Go on a Search ➤ pp. 58-60

The Web is a vast, decentralized collection of millions of sites. You can find pages on topics that interest you by using search services that are free to Internet users. One of the best happens to be offered by AOL itself. It's called NetFind, and you can access it by choosing AOL NetFind from the Internet menu on the toolbar.

Save, Copy, or Print a Web Page ➤ p. 61

Find something on the Web that you'd like to keep? No problem. Use the Save As function on the AOL File menu to save the page either

as an HTML file that can be viewed in your browser or as a text file
that can be used in a word processor. You can also copy and paste text
from a Web page to a text window, or you can print the page, including
graphics, by clicking the Print icon on the toolbar.

Save a Favorite Place ➤ *pp. 61-62*

If you find a Web page that you really like and plan to visit often, go
ahead and save its address using AOL's Favorite Places feature. With
the page displayed on your browser, do one of the following:

- Click the heart on the title bar of the browser and then click
  Add to Favorites to save the address in the Favorite Places
  folder.
- Drag the heart on the browser to the Favorites icon on the
  AOL toolbar.

Create Your Own Web Pages ➤ *pp. 62-64*

With AOL's Personal Publisher, it's easy to create cool-looking
Web pages of your own—and with a few mouse clicks you can also
"publish them" by placing them on a special AOL computer called
My Place, where they'll be available for the whole world to see. To
create a page, do the following:

1. Click Internet on the toolbar and choose Internet Connection.
2. In the Internet Connection window, choose Internet Extras.
3. Click Personal Publisher and then click Create Page.
4. Follow the step-by-step instructions on the screen. It's a cinch!

CREATE A PAGE

When the Internet began to take the world by storm, some commercial online services saw it as a deadly threat. The people at AOL, however, strongly believed that a huge opportunity was at hand. The company launched a drive to integrate its own service with the Internet—and especially with the graphically rich World Wide Web. The campaign has succeeded beyond anyone's expectations. Today, some 40 percent of all activity on the Web goes through AOL. And no wonder: AOL has blended its own content so seamlessly with that of the Web that sometimes it's hard to tell where one stops and the other starts. The marriage is a perfect one for busy people who want the best of an online service and the Internet rolled into one.

What Is the Internet, and Why Is Everybody Using It?

Everybody has heard of the Internet—but it's surprising how many people still don't know exactly what it is. For the record, the Internet is a global network capable of connecting your PC to millions of other computers around the world, including huge mainframes at government agencies and universities as well as the computer systems of major businesses. The Internet began a generation ago as a means of maintaining crucial communications links within the government in case of a nuclear war. As the Cold War lingered on, the Internet languished in obscurity. With the development of the World Wide Web in the 1990s, however, the Internet was transformed. Boasting graphics, photos, animation, and sound in addition to text, the Web let users jump from place to place—even to a computer halfway around the world—with a click of the mouse. Today, consumers get a wide range of information and entertainment from the Web, and it's turning into a fast and efficient way for people to buy goods and services electronically.

DEFINITIONS

Web site: *A collection of Web pages. Web pages are viewed one at a time with a browser.*

Home page: *The first page you see when you visit a Web site.*

URL: *Universal (or uniform) resource locator—a fancy way of saying "Internet address."*

HTTP: *Hypertext transfer protocol—the standard method of transmitting data on the Web. This is one of those examples of technobabble that has made it into the mainstream.*

HTML: *Hypertext markup language—the computer language used to create Web pages. Don't worry; you don't have to know it to use the Internet or AOL.*

Click Your Way onto the Web

With AOL, you can use your mouse to click your way onto the World Wide Web. For example, you can:

- Click the Go to the Web button in the Welcome window. This will take you to AOL's own home page on the Web, a great jumping-off place for browsing and finding stuff.
- Click the little house on the toolbar. This is the Home icon, which will take you to your browser's home page. (As you'll see later in this chapter, you can set AOL to use any page as its home page.)

Before you jump into cyberspace, however, you might want to familiarize yourself with the Web: how it works, and what it has to offer. Reading this chapter should give you the basics. I also recommend that you visit AOL's Internet Connection, which you can access by clicking Internet on the toolbar and then clicking Internet Connection. This area, shown in Figure 3.1, is a good place to start if you're new to the Internet. It gives you easy access to the Web, newsgroups, and other Internet features, as well as to help and information about the Internet in general.

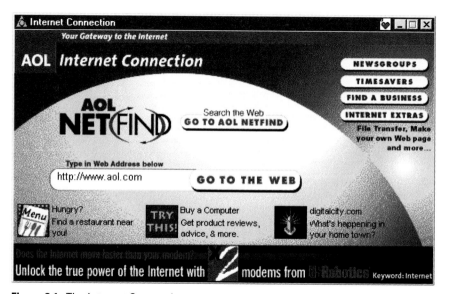

Figure 3.1 The Internet Connection, your gateway to cyberspace

Browser Basics

To use the Web you need a browser—a program that lets you enjoy graphics, animation, photos, and sound as well as text. Fortunately, AOL has a built-in browser. It's a version of the popular Internet Explorer browser developed by Microsoft, and it's totally integrated into the AOL interface. The browser toolbar, shown here, sits below the regular AOL toolbar and is available any time you're online.

Using the Browser Buttons

EXPERT ADVICE

The faster your connection to AOL, the faster you'll be able to surf the Web. Since AOL now supports 56 kbps connections in most areas, it behooves you to get a 56K modem if your computer doesn't already have one.

At the left end of the browser toolbar are some buttons used for Web surfing. Here's what they do:

◁	Back	Takes you back to the last page you visited (either a Web page or an AOL window).
▷	Forward	Takes you forward again one page after you've used the back arrow.
⊗	Stop	Stops the browser in the middle of an operation. If a Web page takes too long to appear, this is a good button to use.
↻	Reload	Refreshes the current page. This is a good tool to use if the page is frequently updated with new information, such as news or sports scores.
⌂	Home	Takes you to your browser's home page.

If you're a diehard Netscape fan, take heart. Newer versions of the Netscape Navigator browser will work with AOL (so, for that matter, will the regular Microsoft Internet Explorer). To use one of these rather than the built-in AOL browser, sign on, minimize the AOL window, and launch the browser.

Keep in mind that the Forward and Back buttons can also be used for AOL windows, not just Web pages.

Internet Addresses

Every Web site has its own unique address, also known as a URL, that lets other computers know where to find it on the Internet. A typical address begins with http://. This is usually followed by www, then a period, and then the actual

Web addresses often include information to the right of the domain name. The extra notation usually indicates a specific page somewhere on a main site. For instance, the address for the page about Web help at AOL's Web site is http://www.aol.com/ nethelp/www/ webaddresses.html.

name of the site. After that is another period (this one's called a dot) and, finally, three letters. Put all these elements together, and you get a name like http:// www.aol.com, which happens to be the address for AOL's home on the Web.

What's in a Name? Domains, That's What.

The three-letter extension at the end of a Web address is called the domain name. This denotes the type of organization at that address, and it's extremely useful in telling you what kind of site you're dealing with. The most common top-level domains are:

.com	Companies
.net	Internet service providers
.edu	Educational institutions
.mil	Military
.org	Nonprofit organizations
.gov	Government

The most heavily used domain of all is .com (pronounced *dot-com*), which consists of sites that are involved in business, whether or not they actually conduct business on the Web. With thousands of companies now advertising their Web addresses on TV as well as in newspapers and magazines, Web addresses are becoming commonplace.

Accessing a Web Address

If you know the address of the site you want to visit, there are several ways to access it (that's not surprising, since there are several ways to do almost everything on AOL). Here are the main ones:

When you use the address space on the toolbar, you can start an address with www. But when you use the keyword feature or enter an address in the Internet Connection window, you need to begin with http://.

- In the Internet Connection window, type the address and click Go to the Web.
- If you know the Internet address you want to reach, just type it in the address space on the toolbar and click Go or press ENTER.
- Click Keyword on the toolbar, or press CTRL-K and enter the address as if it were a keyword.

CAUTION

You don't have to worry about capitalizing proper names in a Web address—use all lowercase if you want to. But you do have to enter addresses exactly right. One missed letter, colon, or slash, and you won't be able to access the site.

Navigating with Hyperlinks

The best thing about the Web is that it lets you jump around from place to place simply by clicking your mouse on hyperlinks—text or graphics with embedded links to other Web addresses. You saw in Chapter 1 that hyperlinks are used within AOL to help you navigate from one area to another. On the Internet, hyperlinks can take you elsewhere within a Web site or to another site halfway around the world. You'll know that text or a graphic is a link if the cursor turns into a hand when you point at that item.

SHORTCUT

From time to time you'll run across Web addresses in documents. Rather than trying to remember them, just copy them and paste them into the address space in the browser toolbar.

Keeping Track of Where You've Been

As you surf the Web, the AOL browser keeps track of the pages you've visited during your current session. This is helpful because it lets you revisit places without having to reenter their addresses or search for them again. To view the last 25 places you've visited (both on AOL and the Web), click the downward-pointing arrow at the right side of the Web address space on the toolbar. You'll see a drop-down list like the one shown in Figure 3.2. Clicking any site in the list will take you directly there.

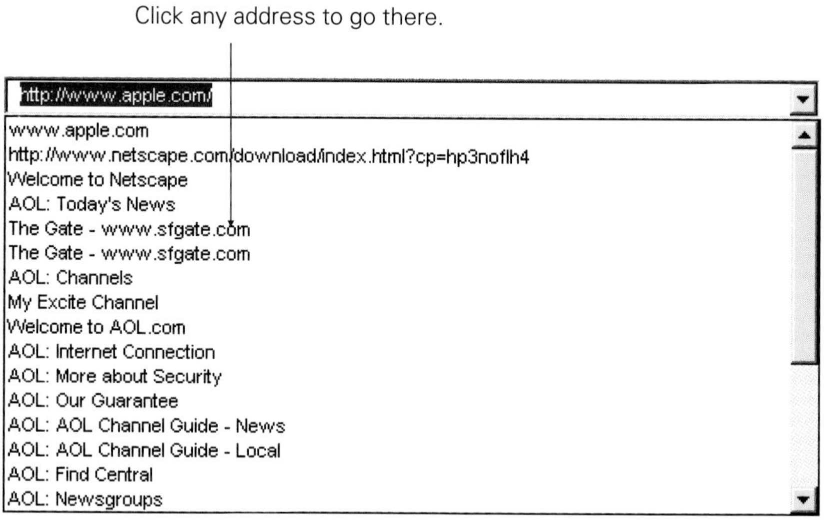

Click any address to go there.

Figure 3.2 Revisiting places you've been is a snap.

Searching the Web with NetFind

Even seasoned Web surfers memorize only a small number of addresses, and busy people certainly have better things to do. Fortunately, you don't have to know a site's address to find it. Just use AOL's NetFind feature. This is an easy-to-use, robust search engine that can direct you to almost any destination on the Web. To use NetFind, follow the instructions in the step-by-step box over on page 59.

For example, suppose you're looking for information about lyme disease, an affliction carried by deer ticks that can cause all sorts of problems in people, including arthritis. Searching for "lyme disease" with NetFind turns up more than 363,000 Web pages with references to it. To help you narrow things down, the most relevant sites are listed first. Better yet, the search results lead off with a section labeled "Try These First," where you'll find one or more really pertinent sites.

An Online Directory at Your Fingertips

In addition to letting you search for a name or topic on the Web, NetFind provides a directory of categories under the heading "Time Savers" that helps you

STEP BY STEP Searching the Web

① **Choose AOL NetFind from the Internet menu to open the AOL NetFind window.**

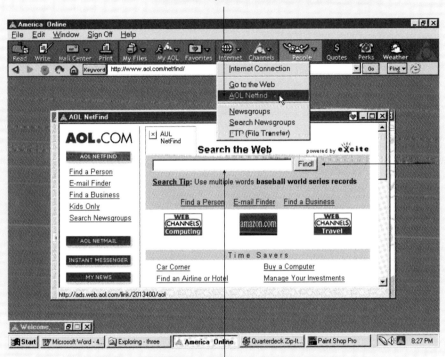

③ **Click here to launch the search and display the results.**

② **Enter a term or brief description of what you're searching for.**

narrow a search. For example, in the "Your Government" category, you'll be able to find the nearest DMV or passport office or get information on national parks.

Other Search Services

Although AOL promotes NetFind, there are lots of other search engines out there that you can use on the Web. Here are a few of the best, along with their Web addresses:

Hotbot	http://www.hotbot.com
Infoseek	http://www.infoseek.com
Excite	http://www.excite.com
Yahoo	http://www.yahoo.com

One of the most popular search services is Yahoo, shown in Figure 3.3. Yahoo was started by two Stanford University students who took their young company public and are now both multimillionaires. Maybe that helps explain the remark by Microsoft's Bill Gates (the richest private citizen on earth), who has referred to the Internet as a "gold rush."

Click to view topics within any category.

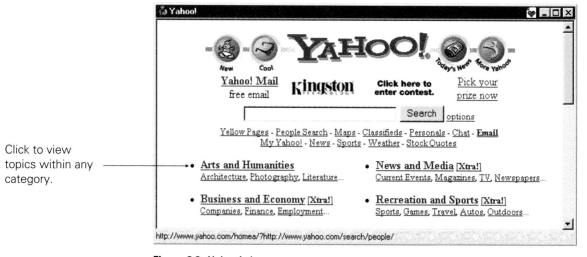

Figure 3.3 Yahoo's home page

EXPERT ADVICE

Search services all do basically the same thing, but they go about it and display their results in different ways. It's a good idea to give all the big ones a try. You may find that one serves your needs better than the others.

Saving, Copying, and Printing Stuff from the Web

Let's say you find something so cool on the Web that you'd like to save it. AOL gives you several options:

- **Save it as a file.** With the Web page displayed, choose Save As from the File menu. Then click the Save as Type box and choose the format you want. You can save the page as an HTML file, which preserves it as a Web page so you can view it again in the browser, or you can save it as a text file, without graphics, which can be used in a word processor.

- **Copy all or part of it.** Use your mouse to select text in the page and then choose Copy from the Edit menu. Open a new text box by choosing New from the File menu and then click Paste on the Edit menu to insert the text.

- **Print it.** To print a Web page, just click Print on the toolbar.

Saving Web Sites as Favorite Places

Wouldn't it be great if you could save the addresses of pages you really like so that you could access them any time you want? The folks at AOL already thought of that. They've incorporated their Favorite Places feature into the Web browser. Let's say you want to add the Netscape Communications home page to your list of Favorite Places. To add a Web page to your list of Favorite Places, do one of the following:

- With the page displayed on the screen, click the heart near the right end of the browser's title bar. Then click Add to Favorites.

- Drag the heart from the title bar to the Favorite Places folder on the AOL toolbar.

In either case, the Netscape address is now safely tucked away among your Favorite Places, as you can see here:

Favorite Places correspond to the bookmarks used by Web browsers such as Netscape Navigator. So now when someone uses the term "bookmark," you'll know what that person means.

Wherever you are in AOL, you can open the Favorite Places folder and double-click the name of a Web page. The browser will automatically take you there.

Setting a Different Home Page

During the course of your Web travels, you may find a page that you'd like to have as your browser's home page—the site that appears each time you click the Home button on the toolbar. Personally, I use as my home page My Excite, a customizable page from Excite (http://www.excite.com) that gives me breaking news plus quotes for stocks I follow and scores for my favorite teams. Yahoo and Infoseek also let you customize personal pages. To change your home page, do the following:

1. Choose Preferences from the My AOL menu on the toolbar and click WWW to display the dialog box shown in Figure 3.4.
2. In the address space under Home Page, enter the name of the page you want: for example, **www.sfgate.com**.
3. Click OK at the bottom of the window.

You'll notice there are three options below the address space. The first, Use Current, is dimmed. You can't use it, so don't try. The second, Use Default, makes Microsoft's home page your home page. The third, Use Blank, gives you no home page, just a blank white screen.

Create Your Own Web Site

The Internet is an interactive experience, and what better way to interact than to create your own Web site. With a site of your own, you can make information about you, your family, your business, and your hobbies available to

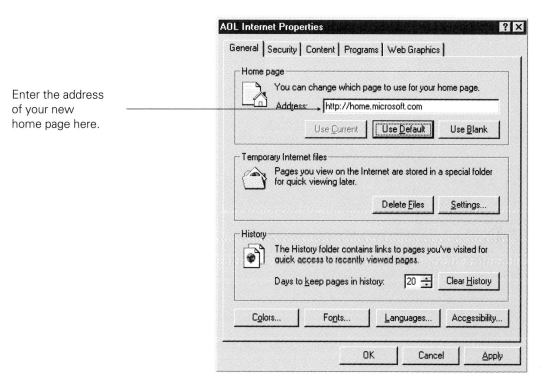

Enter the address
of your new
home page here.

Figure 3.4 Use this Preferences box to change your home page.

anyone else out there in Web land. AOL makes it easy with Personal Publisher, shown in Figure 3.5. This program lets you fashion a cool-looking Web site even if you have no knowledge of HTML. Once you finish creating your site, you can quickly "publish" it to a special area of AOL's computer called My Place, where it will be available day and night to anyone browsing the Web. And the best part is that there is no charge for this service. It's all part of your AOL membership.

Using Personal Publisher

To access Personal Publisher, do the following:

*America Online is currently
working on a new version of
Personal Publisher, which
may differ in certain respects
from the one described here.*

1. Click Internet on the toolbar and then choose Internet Connection.

2. Click Internet Extras and then click Personal Publisher.

Once you're in Personal Publisher, click Create Page to start the process of developing your own site. The program will walk you through the process of

Click here for
step-by-step
instructions.

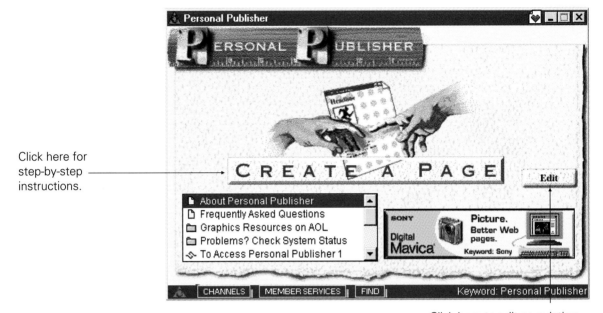

Click here to edit an existing
page or build one from scratch.

Figure 3.5 Use Personal Publisher to create your own Web site.

picking out a template as well as adding a background, graphics, headlines, text, and a title that will appear in the menu bar when the page is launched in a Web browser. If you pretty much know what you want, you can use Personal Publisher's Edit window, shown in Figure 3.6, to build a page without the hand-holding you get in the walk-through. And if you're really ambitious, you can design your page using HTML code, which gives you more sophisticated design options.

EXPERT ADVICE

The information in the title bar of a Web page is what search services key on when they go looking for Web sites—so be sure your title includes your name or other information that will lead people to your page.

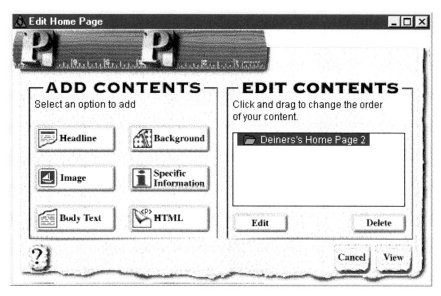

Figure 3.6 Be bold! Design a Web page from scratch.

How Many Pages Can I Have?

The good news is there's no limit to the number of pages you can create. The bad news is you're limited to 2 megabytes of space on the AOL My Place server computer. If you keep your graphics to a minimum, you can have several pages. That's a good idea anyway, because a page heavy with graphics takes a long time to load, and nobody's going to stick around forever to watch your page appear (most big corporations now keep the graphics down on their pages for just that reason).

Downloading Stuff from the Web

In Chapter 7 you'll learn how to download free and cheap software directly from AOL's vast software libraries. Right now, however, let's take a moment to discuss software that can be downloaded from the Internet. You can get thousands of different shareware programs off the Web including useful stuff such as:

• Updated utility software for printers and modems

- The latest and greatest Web browsers from Netscape and Microsoft
- Versions of new software that you can try for free

Many computer and software companies, in fact, now have Web pages devoted to downloadable software.

Go Ahead and Download

Downloading off the Web is a no-brainer. Most Web sites will walk you through the process, and when you indicate you want to download a file, a Windows dialog box like the one shown in Figure 3.7 will appear showing you the name of the file and where it will be saved on your hard disk. You just click Save and sit back and let the computer do its stuff.

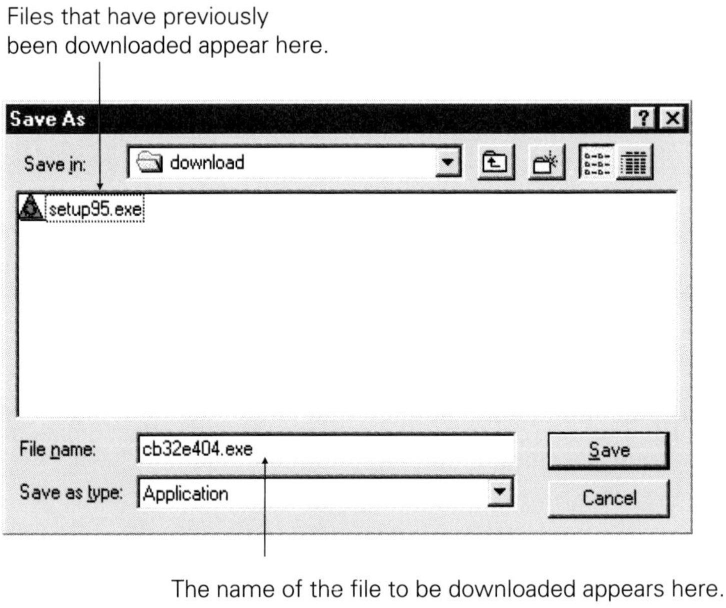

Files that have previously
been downloaded appear here.

The name of the file to be downloaded appears here.

Figure 3.7 This dialog box lets you download and save a file.

But Be Careful...

The bane of every computer user is the computer virus, and some of these digital bugs can be transmitted to your PC over telephone lines, via e-mailed

CAUTION

Even with a fast modem, large programs such as Web browsers can take up to an hour to download. Be sure to factor the time into your plans, because you won't be able to do anything else online while the download is taking place.

documents and downloaded files. As a rule of thumb, make sure your computer is equipped with good software for detecting and eliminating viruses before you download files from the Internet. To find out how to prevent unwanted virus infections, check out Neighborhood Watch (keyword **neighborhood watch**). This area, shown in Figure 3.8, offers information and tools that let you protect your computer (as well as quick access to Parental Controls and ways to block electronic junk mail). You can even get a free trial version of Dr. Solomon's Anti-Virus program.

Figure 3.8 Learn about viruses at Neighborhood Watch.

Shopping on the Internet

If you're concerned about what your kids might find when they're surfing the Web, you can limit their access using AOL's Parental Controls (keyword parental controls). You can choose from four levels of Web access: kids only (ages 12 and under), young teens (ages 13 to 15), mature teens (ages 16 to 17), and adults (ages 18 and older).

As we'll see in the final chapter of this book, shopping via AOL can be wonderfully convenient and enjoyable. But don't limit your online excursions to AOL's Shopping channel. The Web itself is becoming a virtual marketplace bigger than the Mall of America. Most big retailers and catalog merchants now let you buy products directly from their Web sites. Buying something online takes just a few minutes and, in many cases, you can get confirmation of your purchase via e-mail.

Concerned about Security? Don't Be.

- Internet shopping is accomplished with state-of-the-art security technology that encrypts your credit card information during transmission so that no one can steal it. In fact, shopping online is as safe as giving your credit card number to someone over the telephone, and a lot less dangerous than giving your card to a waiter at a restaurant.

If You Ever Need Help

After finishing this chapter, you should be an expert on using the Web—well, maybe not, but if you need more help, you don't have far to look. The folks at AOL have provided some of the best information about the Web that you'll find anywhere. For a general education on the Web and Web terminology, try this:

1. Open the Internet Connection window by choosing Internet Connection from the Internet menu on the toolbar.
2. Click the button for Internet Extras and then click Internet Help, which takes you to the NetHelp page on AOL's own Web site.
3. Scroll down and click the WWW hyperlink.

For specific help and advice about how to use the Web on AOL, use the keyword **help**, which takes you to AOL Member Services, and then click Internet & World Wide Web to display the window shown in Figure 3.9.

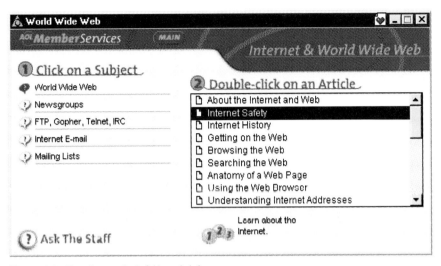

Figure 3.9 Need more help? Here it is!

EXPERT ADVICE

If you really want to get the most out of the Internet, try reading The Official AOL Internet Guide *(Windows edition by David Peal, Mac edition by Kevin Savetz and David Peal), or* The Internet for Busy People, Second Edition, *a brilliant tome by Christian Crumlish. All of these books are published by Osborne/McGraw-Hill, the same folks who brought you the book you're now holding.*

CHECK POINT

The World Wide Web may be grabbing all the headlines, but there's another Internet-related feature of AOL that you might find at least as useful. It's e-mail, the communications phenomenon of the 1990s—and it's the subject of our next chapter.

E-Mail: Corresponding Has Never Been Easier

INCLUDES

- Composing and sending messages
- Using the Address Book
- Attaching files to messages
- Reading new mail
- Sending replies
- Writing offline
- Using Automatic AOL

FAST FORWARD

Compose an Electronic Mail Message ➤ pp. 76-77

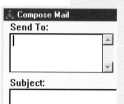

1. Click Write on the toolbar to display the Compose Mail window.
2. Fill in the e-mail address of the recipient.
3. Enter a description of the message in the Subject box.
4. Write your message.
5. Click Send Now.

Put an Address in the Address Book ➤ pp. 78-79

1. Click Mail Center on the toolbar and the choose Address Book.
2. Click the button labeled New Person.
3. Enter the person's real name and e-mail address in the spaces provided.
4. Click OK.

Attach a File to a Message ➤ pp. 80-82

1. Click Write on the toolbar to display the Compose Mail window.
2. Click the button labeled Attachments.
3. Click Attach and then locate the file you want using the dialog box.
4. Click OK. The name of the attached file will appear in the Compose Mail window.
5. Send the message. A copy of the file will be transferred with it.

Check Your Mail ➤ pp. 83-85

1. If you have new mail waiting for you, a voice will announce "You've got mail" when you sign on to AOL. Also, you'll see a notification in the Welcome window, and the flag will be up on the mailbox on the toolbar. Any time you want to read your mail, click Read on the toolbar or click the mailbox in the Welcome window.
2. Click the tab for the kind of mail you want to read—New Mail, Old Mail, or Sent Mail, which is mail you've written and sent.
3. To read a message, select it and click the button labeled Read.

Reply to a Message ➤ pp. 87-88

1. While the message is on the screen, click the Reply button. To include material from the original message, select the text you want before clicking Reply.
2. Write your response and click Send Now.

Write a Message Offline ➤ p. 89

1. Before you sign on, click Write on the toolbar.
2. Write and address your message just as you would if you were online.
3. Instead of clicking Send Now, click Send Later.
4. Sign on. A small window will appear notifying you that you have mail waiting to be sent. Click Send Now.

Let AOL Send and Get Your Mail Automatically ➤ pp. 89-92

1. Click Mail Center and choose Set up Automatic AOL (Flashsessions).
2. Choose the option for getting unread mail.
3. Click the Schedule Automatic AOL button and then set the times for your PC to automatically sign on and check for mail.
4. Select the box labeled Enable Scheduler. Now Automatic AOL will periodically sign you on, check and send mail, and then sign you off, thus saving time.

Despite the enormous growth of the World Wide Web, it's not the most widely used feature of the Internet. That distinction belongs to electronic mail, or e-mail, as it is popularly known. E-mail is such a widespread phenomenon that it has entered the language as a noun, a verb, and an adjective. It has become an indispensable tool in the workplace, and almost every business card now includes an e-mail address. But it's also great for personal correspondence. Using e-mail is more convenient than writing and mailing a letter, and it even has advantages over the telephone—you needn't worry that the person won't be there, time zones aren't a problem, and you don't have to deal with voicemail. In short, it's ideal for busy people.

Anyone, Anywhere, Any Time

You can use America Online's e-mail feature to exchange messages with other AOL members or with anyone in the world who has an e-mail address. You can send and receive messages any time, day or night. And there's no extra charge for sending e-mail—it's included in your membership rate. A few special features are available when you're writing to another AOL member, as you'll see later in this chapter, but you use the same basic techniques to communicate via e-mail no matter who's on the other end of your message.

DEFINITION

Mail: A term used by AOL's software to refer to e-mail. It's okay to use mail
and e-mail interchangeably. In fact, I think I'll do that.

Everyone who uses e-mail has a unique e-mail address. When you correspond with other AOL members, you can simply use your screen name—but when
you go out on the Internet, you need a full-fledged Internet address so that people
using other online services or Internet accounts can send you mail. Your full
Internet address is your screen name followed by @aol.com, as in Dein-
eis@aol.com (that's me).

The Mail Center:
AOL's Version of Your Local Post Office

There are various ways to access AOL's e-mail functions and, as with other
AOL features, there's a good deal of redundancy. A good way to get started is to
go to the Mail Center. Click its icon on the toolbar and then choose Mail Center
to open the Mail Center window, shown in Figure 4.1.

As you can see, not only can you use this window as a gateway for reading
and writing mail, it's also a perfect spot to come for help—assuming you still need
any after you finish this chapter. However, there are quicker ways to get things

*AOL often gives you several
ways to do the same thing.
For instance, you can open
the Compose Mail window by
clicking the Mail Center icon
and then choosing Write.
Pick the shortcuts that are
best for a busy person like
yourself.*

Figure 4.1 The Mail Center: Everything in one place

done than going to the Mail Center. To compose a new e-mail message, for example, you can:

- Click Write on the toolbar.
- Press the Ctrl key and the letter M at the same time.

Either way, the Compose Mail window will pop up. This is a lot easier than hunting up a piece of paper, a pen, an envelope, and a stamp.

Composing Your Message

Writing a simple message (or even an extraordinarily erudite one) involves just a few steps. A short message, in fact, can be composed and sent off in a minute or two. Just open the Compose Mail window and follow the step-by-step instructions.

STEP BY STEP Writing an E-mail Message

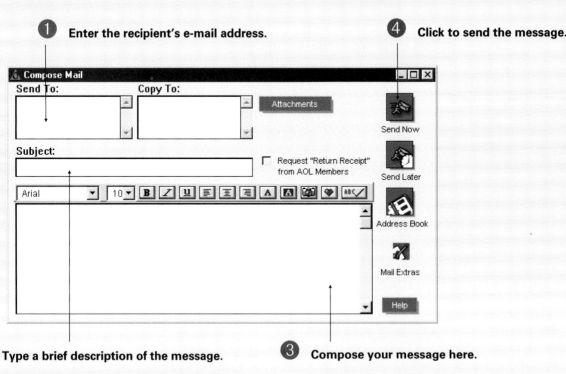

① **Enter the recipient's e-mail address.**

④ **Click to send the message.**

② **Type a brief description of the message.**

③ **Compose your message here.**

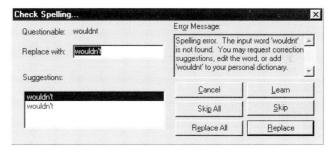

SHORTCUT

You can send the same message to more than one person simultaneously. Just enter addresses one after the other, separating them with commas. This technique works in both the Send To box and the Copy To box.

Don't Forget to Check Your Spelling

With Version 4.0 of its software, AOL has added the ability to check spelling in an e-mail message—so you never have to make a fool of yourself online again (at least not by misspelling words). After you compose your message, just click the button labeled ABC on the formatting toolbar above the message. If the software encounters what it thinks is a problem, it will let you know, as in Figure 4.2. In this case, I neglected to put an apostrophe in the word "wouldn't." I shouldn't have done that. Fortunately, with the AOL spell checker, it's easy to fix.

Need the spelling of a word or a quick definition? No problem. Just choose Dictionary or Thesaurus from the main Edit window. You can do this while composing a message or from any other point in AOL.

Figure 4.2 Misspelled words are a thing of the past.

Okay, Now Send It!

When you've finished writing your missive, send it by clicking the Send Now button at the right side of the window. If all goes smoothly, you'll see a box telling you that your mail has been sent. (If it's a really important message to another AOL member, you might want to check the Return Receipt option before sending. That way, you'll get confirmation that your message has been received (this does not work for Internet addresses—only for AOL members).

Mail from one AOL member to another is handled by AOL's own computer system and is supposed to arrive in seconds. Mail sent across the Internet from an AOL member to a nonmember or vice versa can take much, much longer. Some people report it can even take days. It doesn't mean you mail is lost — just slow.

Check Mail You've Sent

To reread a message you've e-mailed to someone, choose the Sent Mail tab in your Mailbox window, or click Mail Center on the toolbar and choose Sent Mail. In addition to reading sent mail, you can do a couple of other nifty things—but only if the message was sent to another AOL member; the following features don't work on Internet mail:

- Click the Status button to see if and when your message was read by the recipient.
- Click the Unsend button to retrieve a message after you've sent it. Note that this works only if the message has not yet been read by the recipient.

EXPERT ADVICE

Write messages to yourself to practice using e-mail. You'll find out how different procedures look to recipients, and you'll always have a pen pal you can rely on. (Seriously, using your own account to test e-mail is a great idea.)

The Address Book

E-mail addresses can be difficult to remember. Not to worry, however. AOL has a feature called the Address Book in which you can keep frequently used addresses and retrieve them with a click of the mouse. To store addresses, open the Address Book, shown in Figure 4.3, by clicking Mail Center on the toolbar and then choosing Address Book.

To add an entry to your Address Book, click the New Person button. This will bring up the dialog box shown in Figure 4.4, where you enter the person's name and e-mail address. After completing the form, click OK to add the entry to the Address book. Now you can easily address an e-mail message. Just open the Address Book, select the name you want, and click Send To. A fresh Compose Mail window will appear, automatically addressed.

You can also include a photo of a person along with their address — putting a face together with a name can be helpful. To do that you must have a digital image of the photo in an .art, .jpg, .gif or .bmp format. To include a photo, click the Picture Tab in the address form, then click Select Picture, locate the photo and double-click it.

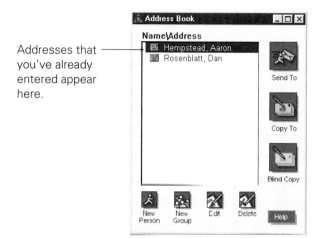

Addresses that you've already entered appear here.

Figure 4.3 The Address Book window

EXPERT ADVICE

You can easily send mail to a group of people. Instead of adding multiple addresses in the Send To box of the Compose Mail window, create a group entry in the Address Book: click New Group and then enter the e-mail addresses for everyone in the group.

Click here to include a photo with the address.

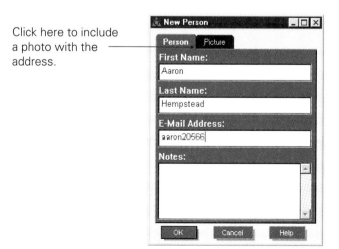

Figure 4.4 The form for entering addresses

Attaching Files to Your Mail

Sometimes you may want to send someone a spreadsheet or the draft of a report. No problem. You can send text documents, graphics, or any other files by attaching them to an e-mail message. Here's how to attach a file:

1. Open the Compose Mail window, fill in the address and subject boxes, and write your message.
2. Click the Attachments button. This opens a dialog box that lets you search your hard disk to find the file you want to attach.
3. Once you've located the file, it will appear in the Attachments dialog box, as shown here:

Repeat the process if you want to attach other files. Click OK to attach the files to your e-mail. (If you include multiple attachments in a message, they'll automatically be compressed into a zip file so they can be sent faster.)

When you send the message, a copy of the attached file will be transmitted along with it. (Don't worry; the original file remains undisturbed on your hard disk.)

Keep in mind that there are limits to the size of mail that can be sent. You can send up to 2 megabytes to another AOL member, but only 1 megabyte to someone on the Internet.

Dress Up Your Writing

When you're writing to someone out in Internet-land, you're limited to plain text for your message. But if the recipient is an AOL member, you can make

CAUTION

In theory, sending attached files is a piece of cake. In reality, it can present problems, especially if you want to send complex data and graphics. Before you send a file, make sure the recipient has software capable of viewing and editing it.

your prose a lot more colorful, as you can see in Figure 4.5. Most busy people probably have better things to do than send a green and pink electronic mailgram, but the capability's there if you want it. Hey, I don't invent this stuff—I just write about it! Anyway, to apply attributes to text (boldface, underlining, italics) or to change its alignment or its color, do the following:

1. Select the text you want to change.
2. Click the appropriate button on the formatting toolbar, located just above the writing area in the Compose Mail window.

Share Your Favorite Places

Got a favorite place you'd like to share with another AOL member? No problem. Just drag the place marker from your Favorite Places folder (or drag the

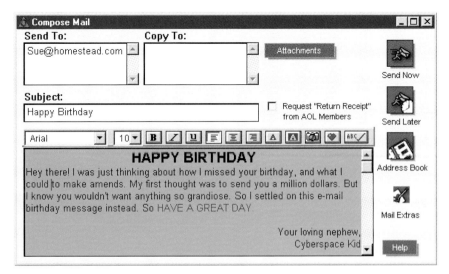

Figure 4.5 A pleasant message that's a little hard on the eyes

heart from the title bar of any window) and drop it into an e-mail message (you can open the Favorite Places folder directly from the Compose Mail window by clicking the heart in the toolbar above the writing area). The place marker appears in the message as a hyperlink. When the recipient opens the message, he or she can click it and go right to the favorite place. Cool or what?

Get Fancy; Add a Piece of Art If you really want to impress a fellow AOL member, add a photo or graphic to your e-mail message. Just click the camera icon in the formatting toolbar of the Compose Mail window and then locate the file of the image (you must have first saved it on your hard disk). For example, check out the photo of Demi Moore in "G.I. Jane" that I've inserted in Figure 4.6. (Note that only users of AOL 4.0 will see the picture. Users of the previous version will see the message "Unable to display AOL 4.0 image.")

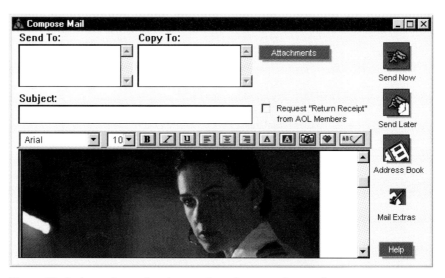

Figure 4.6 A picture is worth a thousand words—even in e-mail.

EXPERT ADVICE

While on the road with your notebook PC, you can back up files you create by sending them to yourself as e-mail attachments. This is also a good way to transfer files between your PC at home and your computer at the office.

You've Got Mail!

Whenever you sign on to AOL, you'll know right away whether there's new e-mail waiting for you. In fact, you won't be settled in your chair before you find out, because an assertive male voice will begin your AOL session with the announcement, "You've got mail!" And if a new message arrives while you're online, you'll get the same audio alert, plus the flag on the mailbox on the toolbar will go up. So basically, you have no excuse for not reading your mail. You certainly can't say, "Gosh, I didn't realize you'd sent me an e-mail."

Reading Your Mail

The easiest way to peruse your mail is to click Read on the toolbar. This will display the Mailbox window shown in Figure 4.7. By default, you'll see a list of messages that you haven't read yet, but you also can display a list of old messages you've already read, and messages you've sent by choosing the tabs labeled Old Mail and Sent Mail.

Click to see mail you've already read.

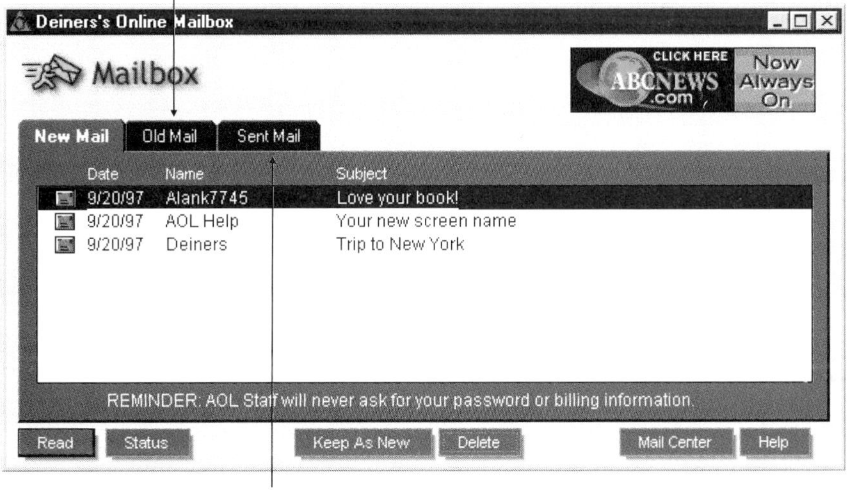

Click to see messages you've sent.

Figure 4.7 Your AOL mailbox keeps track of all your messages.

At the bottom of the window are some buttons. Here's what the key ones do:

- **Read** Opens the message so you can read it.
- **Keep As New** Keeps the message in the New Mail box.
- **Delete** Gets rid of the message. Think twice before using this one.

If you decide to read the message, it will be displayed as in the example in Figure 4.8. This is a message I wrote and sent to myself.

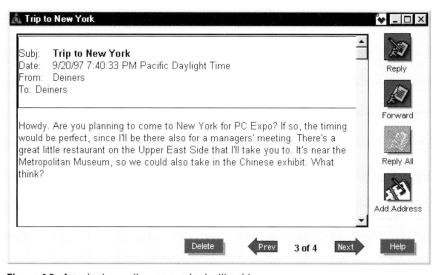

Figure 4.8 A typical e-mail message looks like this.

SHORTCUT

Whenever you have more than one piece of new mail, you can go from the current one to the next one just by clicking the Next button in the bottom-right corner of the window. This button appears only when you have multiple messages.

Reading an Attachment

You'll know that your mail includes an attachment if two buttons—Download File and Download Later—appear beneath the message, as shown in Figure 4-9.

Check here for details about attachments.

Figure 4.9 Incoming mail with a file attached

Clicking the Download File button will start AOL's Download Manager. Click Save to automatically transfer the file to the Download folder inside the main AOL folder on your hard disk. If you'd rather put the file somewhere else, choose a new destination folder before clicking OK. (For a full explanation of downloading, see Chapter 7.) Once the file's downloaded, you'll be able to read it using an appropriate program. For instance, if the file was created in Microsoft Word, you must open it in a program that can display Word documents.

CAUTION

E-mail attachments can carry viruses that can foul up your computer system, so make it a point not to download attachments from strangers.

When you send an attachment from AOL to someone over the Internet, it's automatically encoded using MIME, which stands for Multipurpose Internet Mail Extensions. If the recipient has a MIME-compliant e-mail program, the attachment should come through okay. When you receive a MIME-encoded attached file from an Internet address, the AOL software will decode it for you. If an attachment is garbled, it probably wasn't encoded properly.

Keeping Mail Permanently

By default, AOL deletes mail from your mailbox three days after you read it. You can increase that to seven days using Mail Preferences, as shown in Figure 4.10. Mail that you haven't opened stays in your New Mail box for 35 days before it's dumped.

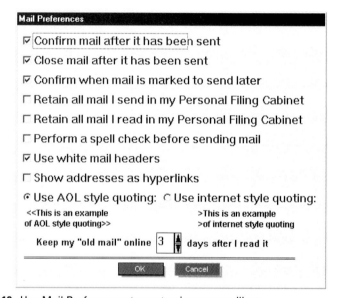

Figure 4.10 Use Mail Preferences to customize your mailbox.

However, there is a way to keep mail that you've read and sent permanently in your Personal Filing Cabinet. Just choose Mail Preferences from the Mail Center menu and check the appropriate boxes. Then, whenever you want to reread your mail, even if you're offline, do the following:

1. Click My Files on the AOL toolbar.
2. Choose Offline Mail to see a list of your stored messages in your Personal Filing Cabinet.
3. Select a message and click Open to read it, or just double-click it.

How to Censor Your Mail

If your children are active online, they probably exchange e-mail with their friends. But suppose there are some individuals or groups that you would rather not have Bobby getting mail from. No problem. With Mail Controls, you can dictate which e-mail addresses will be allowed to exchange messages with any screen name on your AOL account. To set up the controls, click Mail Center on the toolbar and then click Mail Controls and follow the instructions.

Replying to Messages

One of the best things about e-mail is that it lets you easily respond to messages. You can even include all or part of the original message in your reply. To reply to a message, use the following steps:

1. Display the message and then click the Reply button. This opens a new message composition window. The address of the person you're responding to is automatically inserted in the Send To box, and the subject of the original message preceded by "Re:"appears in the Subject box.

2. Write your response just as if you were composing a new message. You can attach a file, use the Address Book, or do anything else you would do with a regular message.

3. When you're finished, click the Send Now button.

EXPERT ADVICE

When you get a message that's really important or that contains information you'll need when you're away from your PC, it's a good idea to print it. To print a message, display it on the screen and then choose Print from the File menu.

Quoting the Original Message

There will probably be times when you will want to include all or part of the original message in a reply, just to remind the other person what he or she wrote about in the first place. Here's how:

1. With the original message on your screen, use your mouse to select the material you want to quote as part of your response.
2. Click the Reply button. A Compose Mail window, like the one in Figure 4.11, will appear that includes the original text you selected.
3. Compose your reply above the quoted material and then click Send Now.

Quoted material
appears this way.

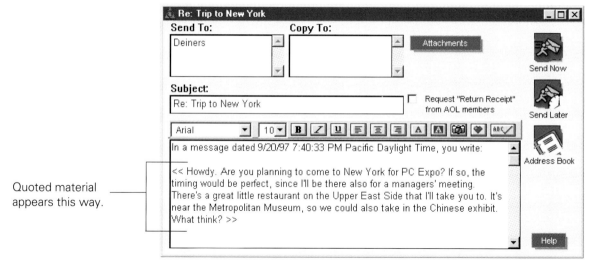

Figure 4.11 The Compose Mail window, including quoted text from the original message

Forwarding Messages

Occasionally you might want to send a message you've received on to a third person. Maybe somebody has e-mailed you a good joke, and you'd like to pass it on to a friend. It's easy. With the original message on your screen, click the Forward button. A new message composition window will appear. All you have to do is enter your friend's e-mail address and click the Send button. (The message itself will not appear, but it will be forwarded—trust me.)

SHORTCUT

When you receive a message from someone with whom you plan to correspond frequently, it's easy to automatically add the person to your Address Book. With the message displayed, just click the button labeled Add Address.

Wait a Minute, Mister Postman...

You don't have to be signed on to AOL to write an e-mail message. In fact, you can compose a message offline the same way you would if you were connected. The Write icon on the toolbar is available when you're offline, as is the Address Book. Compose your message exactly as you would if you were signed on. Then click Send Later, which will save the mail for later delivery. Next time you sign on, AOL will alert you that you have mail waiting to be sent:

To send the mail, simply click Send Now.

Sending Mail with Automatic AOL

As I said earlier, you can't check or send new mail unless you're connected to AOL—but you can have your computer sign on by itself and do those chores for you if you use Automatic AOL. You can set this feature to operate unattended at regular intervals, from once a week to once every 30 minutes. It can also be used to send and retrieve Internet newsgroup postings and download software files. But if you're like most people, you'll probably use this feature primarily to stay on top of your e-mail.

There Are a Few Conditions

For Automatic AOL to work, all of the following conditions must be met:

- Your computer must be turned on.
- The AOL software must be running, and your password must be stored (see Chapter 2 for instructions). You can either leave the sign-on window visible or minimize it and use other programs.
- The PC's internal clock should be set correctly so Automatic AOL can work when it's supposed to.

CAUTION

Automatic AOL is great for busy people, but if you're going to leave your computer unattended, make sure it's in a secure place. If your password is stored, your AOL account is available to anyone who wants to use it.

Configuring Automatic AOL

Click Mail Center on the AOL toolbar and then choose Set Up Automatic AOL (Flashsessions), which will display the window shown in Figure 4.12. You can do this either online or offline.

All the options are right there in front of you. If you're a beginner, you might want to click the Walk Me Through button. This initiates a short step-by-step procedure, during which you'll get to choose the features you want to activate. If you know what you want to do, you can just check the appropriate boxes in the Automatic AOL window and then click Schedule Automatic AOL. This will display the dialog box shown here, which lets you set the times for automatically retrieving and sending mail.

SHORTCUT

Any time you want to sign on, retrieve and/or send mail, and then immediately sign off, just choose Run Automatic AOL (Flashsessions) Now from the Mail Center menu and then click Begin. This operation won't interfere with regularly scheduled Automatic AOL sessions.

Messages retrieved using Automatic AOL sessions also can be found in your Old Mail mailbox online—but they won't show up in your New Mail box, so don't look for them there.

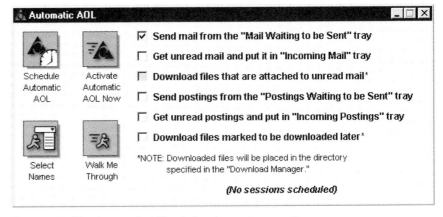

Figure 4.12 The Automatic AOL window lays out your options.

Reading Mail You Receive via Automatic AOL

Mail retrieved during an Automatic AOL session can be read offline, of course. To read your Automatic AOL messages, choose Offline Mail from the My Files menu. This will display a list of messages that have been stored in your Personal Filing Cabinet.

Not Even AOL Is Immune to Junk Mail

You may get a rude shock when you check your mail, because as likely as not, your New Mail box will have some junk mail in it. It could be anything from a sales pitch for a new product to a proposal describing how you can make thousands of dollars a week working at home—in other words, the same sort of junk that fills up your regular mailbox at home. You can reduce your chances of getting junk mail with AOL's Mail Controls, which give you a number of options for specifying who you can send messages to your mailbox. In addition, you can report junk mail abuses, helping the folks at AOL come up with technical and legal ways to battle junk mailers. To access Mail Controls or report junk mail, use the keyword **junk mail**.

Mailing Lists

E-mail isn't just for exchanging messages with individuals. It's also used for Internet mailing lists. Don't be put off by the term—these aren't like regular mailing lists, which are used to spread your name around for marketing purposes. Internet mailing lists are global discussion groups that let e-mail users share information. A mailing list can take the form of an electronic newsletter or a forum for public debate, or it can just be a group of people with common interests. Mailing lists are a good way to stay up-to-date on current issues. And, like most other stuff on the Internet, they're free.

How to Locate Mailing Lists

The place to start if you're interested in mailing lists is the Mailing List Directory window, shown in Figure 4.13. To get there, use the keyword **mailinglists**.

Figure 4.13 The AOL Mailing List Directory

As you can see, AOL gives you access to more than 3,300 mailing lists (the number may have grown by the time you read this). Clicking Browse the Directory will take you to the directory itself, which happens to be located on the World Wide Web. AOL put it there to make it available to anyone with Internet access, not just AOL members. Are these guys thoughtful or what? You can use the directory's index of categories or search by topic to locate names and descriptions of mailing lists.

Most lists let anyone join, but some can get picky, and you may be asked to submit the reasons why you ought to be admitted. (Imagine—snobs on the Internet!) Assuming that your request is approved, you should start receiving messages sent to the list within a day or two.

Subscribing and Unsubscribing

Before you can start receiving messages from a mailing list, you must subscribe to it. This is standard operating procedure, and information on how to subscribe (as well as how to unsubscribe) is routinely included in the description of a list.

Sending Messages to a Mailing List

Most mailing lists welcome participation by subscribers. The e-mail address for posting messages is usually included with the description of the list, along with the subscription information. Note that some lists are edited, which means that somebody decides which messages from subscribers will be sent to the entire list.

CAUTION

You can subscribe to as many mailing lists as you like, but just remember that anything you receive from a mailing list will come to you in the form of e-mail—so it's a good idea to monitor a mailing list at first to make sure it won't clutter up your New Mail box.

CHECK POINT

What's next? More Internet stuff, that's what. In addition to e-mail and the World Wide Web, AOL lets you play around with the exciting, informative, and often controversial world of newsgroups. Stay tuned for a look at how to participate in global discussions on everything from science to skiing.

5

Newsgroups: Your Global Bulletin Board

INCLUDES

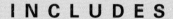

- Subscribing to a newsgroup

- Reading news messages

- Posting news messages and replies

- Using proper netiquette

- Limiting your kids' newsgroup access

FAST FORWARD

Subscribe to a Newsgroup ➤ pp. 100-103

Topics

rec.animals
rec.answers
rec.antiques
rec.aquaria
rec.arts
rec.audio
rec.autos
rec.aviation
rec.backcountry
rec.basketball
rec.beer

To get started using newsgroups, click the Internet button on the toolbar and then choose Newsgroups, or just use the keyword **newsgroups**. Either action opens the Newsgroups window.

- If you know the name of the newsgroup you want to subscribe to, click Expert Add and enter the name. Then click Add.
- To find newsgroups on a specific topic, click Search All Newsgroups, enter a word or phrase, and then click OK. If the search returns a newsgroup you want to subscribe to, select it from the list and click Add.
- If you're a total beginner, try browsing AOL's massive database of newsgroups. Start by clicking Add Newsgroups. If you find a newsgroup you like, select it and click add.

Read a Message ➤ pp. 103-106

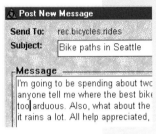

Read My Newsgroups

Read Offline

Add Newsgroups

1. Click Read My Newsgroups in the Newsgroups window.
2. In the list of the newsgroups you've subscribed to, highlight the one that contains messages you want to read and click List Unread. You will be presented with a list of all the items you haven't yet seen.
3. To read a message, highlight the subject and click Read.

Post a Message ➤ pp. 106-110

Post New Message

Send To: rec.bicycles.rides
Subject: Bike paths in Seattle

Message
I'm going to be spending about two
anyone tell me where the best bike
too arduous. Also, what about the
it rains a lot. All help appreciated,

1. In the Newsgroups window, click Read My Newsgroups and then double-click a newsgroup to access it.
2. Click Send New Message.
3. Enter a description of your message in the Subject box and write your message in the Message area.
4. Click Send to post the message to the newsgroup.

Read Messages Offline ➤ pp. 110-111

You can use Automatic AOL to have your computer automatically sign on to AOL and retrieve unread newsgroup messages, which you can then read offline. Here's how:

1. Click Read Offline in the Newsgroups window.
2. In the dialog box that appears, either click Add All or select the desired newsgroup and click Add. When you've finished adding newsgroups, click OK.
3. Choose Set Up Automatic AOL from the Mail menu.
4. Select the box Get Unread Postings and Put in "Incoming Postings" Tray.
5. The next time Automatic AOL is activated, all unread messages in the groups you've selected will be downloaded to your Personal Filing Cabinet.

Set Preferences ➤ pp. 111-113

Click Set Preferences in the main Newsgroups window to display customization options. You can use the Preferences dialog box to create a personalized "signature" that you can append to messages you send. You can also change the order in which new incoming messages appear.

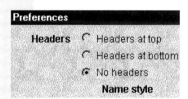

E-mail isn't the only method of exchanging information over the Internet. There are also global forums called newsgroups that let you post and read messages about particular topics—messages that can be read by millions of computer users. Newsgroups can be an invaluable tool for busy people. A friend of mine whose passion is scuba diving uses newsgroups to scope out great locations for scuba vacations. And people I know in the computer business keep on top of the latest trends through newsgroups, which have given a whole new meaning to the phrase "news travels fast." Newsgroups are similar to America Online's internal Message Boards, but they aren't hampered by AOL's rigid restrictions on language and subject matter. We'll talk about the Message Boards in Chapter 6. Right now, let's take a look at the wild and woolly world of newsgroups.

Something for Everyone

Newsgroups, known collectively as Usenet, cover nearly every subject you can imagine, from cats to computers and from politics to poker. New groups are being added daily, and AOL does its best to keep up with the rush. You can get started using newsgroups in a couple of ways:

- Click Internet on the toolbar and then choose Newsgroups from the menu.
- Use the keyword **newsgroups**.

Either of these procedures will take you to the main Newsgroups window, shown in Figure 5.1.

This list offers helpful resources
related to newsgroups.

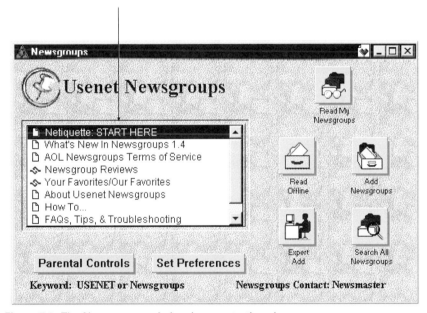

Figure 5.1 The Newsgroups window is your starting place.

DEFINITION

Usenet: *Short for user network, an umbrella term for the Internet newsgroups. There is no central governing body for Usenet, and in fact it would be extremely difficult to govern because it's so big. As of this writing, there are more than 20,000 newsgroups.*

Newsgroup Lingo

Like the World Wide Web, Usenet has its own language. (You didn't know this was a book on linguistics, did you?) Take heart, however: it's a very easy language to learn. Each newsgroup has a name composed of several parts, separated by periods, that together determine the newsgroup's identity within Usenet. Here's a typical newsgroup name:

rec.arts.movies.reviews

The first part of the name is its main category, also known as a hierarchy. That's followed by one or more subcategories and finally by a word that denotes the specific subject matter of the group. Here's a rundown of some of the major hierarchies, which contain the most popular newsgroups:

- **rec** Groups involved with recreational interests. This is the most wide-ranging category, encompassing everything from motorcycles to music. If you have a hobby, no matter how obscure, there's probably a newsgroup to accommodate you.

- **comp** Groups that offer computer information. Newsgroups in this category can help you find answers to questions about your hardware and software.

- **alt** "Alternative" groups. The alt category is an immense grab bag of interesting, dull, and even lurid subjects. This is the category that contains the sexually explicit groups.

- **soc** Groups that deal with social issues such as religion, history, and politics.

You Have to Subscribe, but It's Free

To participate in a newsgroup, you must first subscribe to it. (AOL uses the term "adding," which means that you add a newsgroup to the list of the groups you subscribe to.) This is a lot easier than subscribing to a newspaper or a magazine. There are no forms to fill out and mail, no telephone calls to make, and—best of all—no payments. You can subscribe to as many newsgroups as you want—it's absolutely free.

Adding Newsgroups

There are several ways to subscribe to a newsgroup. (There are several ways to do everything on AOL, so why should this be any different?) If you have no idea what you're looking for, try clicking Add Newsgroups in the main Newsgroups window. You will be presented with AOL's database of newsgroups. Clicking a hierarchy will give you a list of topics. Bear in mind, though, that the selection is enormous. Figure 5.2 shows the first part of a list of 95 newsgroups dealing with music in the rec hierarchy.

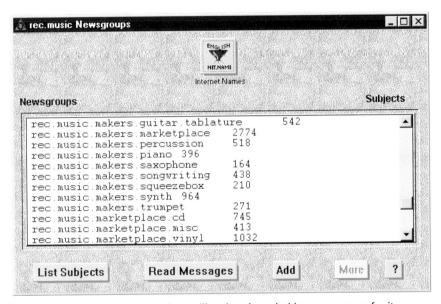

Figure 5.2 No matter what music you like, there's probably a newsgroup for it.

EXPERT ADVICE

You can't send a message to a newsgroup until you've subscribed to it, but you can read messages in newsgroups that you view via Add Newsgroups. This is a useful way to get a feel for a newsgroup before you decide whether to add it to your list.

Searching for Newsgroups

A second option is to use the Search All Newsgroups feature. This presents you with a dialog box in which you enter words or phrases that describe a topic that interests you. Although this feature can be a helpful tool, it has its limits because it finds only those newsgroups that have the words or designations you specify in their names. That's great in some cases—you'll find more than 150 groups devoted to IBM, for instance—but try searching for science fiction, and you'll come up empty. That's because science fiction newsgroups are denoted by "sf"—and if you try searching for sf you'll get the mishmash shown in Figure 5.3, which includes stuff on the San Francisco 49ers and on Bakersfield, California.

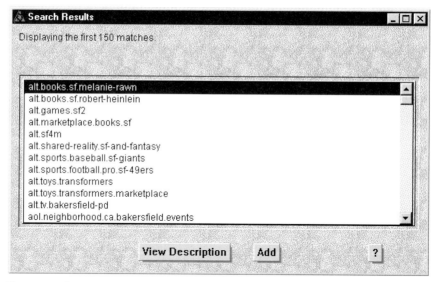

Figure 5.3 Searching for newsgroups can be frustrating!

EXPERT ADVICE

The names of newsgroups can be cryptic, but AOL can help: wherever you see a button labeled Internet Names or View Description, highlight the name of a newsgroup and click the button for a description of the group in plain English.

The Expert Approach

If you know the name of the newsgroup you want to subscribe to, you can use the Expert Add feature:

1. Click Expert Add in the Newsgroups window.
2. Enter the name of the newsgroup. Be absolutely precise, because one misplaced period or misspelled word will prevent the Expert Add feature from locating the newsgroup and adding it to your list. (It may be expert, but it's not very smart.)
3. Click Add.

EXPERT ADVICE

AOL has deliberately omitted sexually explicit and other controversial newsgroups from the database that's connected to Add Newsgroups and Search All Newsgroups—but with Expert Add, you can add any group that's out there.

Your Newsgroup List

Once you've subscribed to a newsgroup, you can read messages that other people have written, and you can post your own. (By the way, newsgroup messages are also called articles and posts.) Clicking Read My Newsgroups in the Newsgroups window displays a window like the one shown in Figure 5.4 showing the groups to which you are subscribed.

You'll notice that your newsgroup list includes several newsgroups that you didn't subscribe to. AOL took the liberty of adding them for you. They include groups that pertain to AOL itself, along with groups that deal with Usenet issues.

If You Don't Like It, Dump It!

It's even easier to unsubscribe to a newsgroup than it is to subscribe to one. Any time you get tired of a group, highlight it in your newsgroup list and click Remove. You can subscribe and unsubscribe to newsgroups as often as you like.

Perusing a Newsgroup

Messages in newsgroups are listed by subject. To display a list of subjects in a newsgroup, select the group in the Read My Newsgroup window and then click List Unread or List All to display a window like the one shown in Figure 5.5.

Click to see descriptions of
newsgroups in plain English.

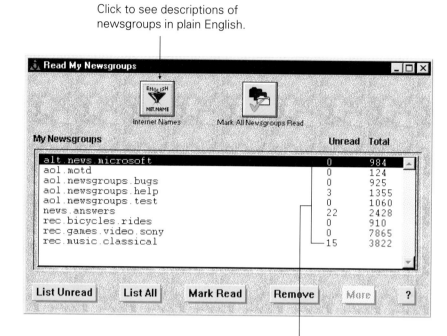

This column shows the number of
messages you haven't looked at.

Figure 5.4 Here's the way your newsgroups are listed.

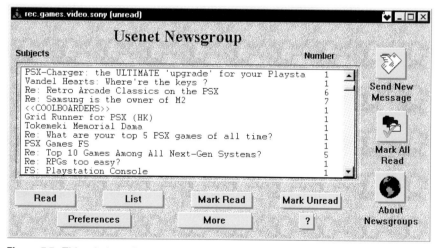

Figure 5.5 This window shows subjects under discussion in a newsgroup.

(Choosing List Unread will show you only the items that you haven't already looked at.)

SHORTCUT

Use the cursor keys on your keyboard to move quickly through long lists of subjects. The PAGE UP and PAGE DOWN keys move you a screenful of items at a time, and HOME and END take you directly to the first and final entries, respectively.

Avoiding Message Overload

Suppose you don't want to sift through dozens, hundreds, or even thousands of messages in a newsgroup—you just want to read messages that have been posted since you last checked out the group. No problem. Highlight the newsgroup in the Read My Newsgroups window and click Mark Read. All of the messages currently in the group will be given the bum's rush so that the next time you go to read your newsgroup, they won't be there. You can even mark all your newsgroups as read (with the Mark All Newsgroups Read button), which will let you start fresh with all your newsgroups the next time you sign on.

EXPERT ADVICE

Once you mark an entire newsgroup as read, you can't undo the procedure—but it is possible to reverse the damage. Simply remove the newsgroup from your list and then resubscribe to it. All the items in the group will reappear, just like that!

Reading and Writing Messages

Okay, put on your reading glasses, because it's time to get down to business. To peruse newsgroup messages, select the subject you want to explore and click Read. If the subject contains more than one message, you'll see the message that began the thread. A newsgroup message looks a lot like an e-mail message (see Figure 5.6). It shows you who wrote it and when it was sent. It also may include text quoted from another message to which the author is responding.

You'll see information about who
posted the message and when.

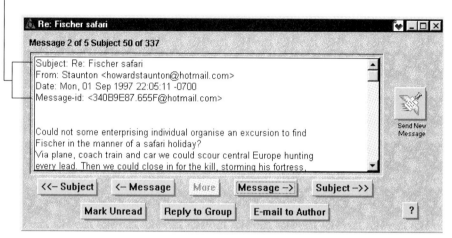

Figure 5.6 A typical newsgroup message looks like this.

*As the Internet becomes
more commercialized, many
newsgroups have turned
into dumping grounds for
messages advertising
products and services. This
isn't the way things were
supposed to be, but there
doesn't seem to be any way
of stopping this trend.*

Okay, Now It's Your Turn...

Once you get comfortable reading newsgroup messages, you probably will want to join the millions of users who post messages every day. You can use newsgroups to request information or opinions from other users, or you can put in your own two cents' worth in response to other messages.

But First, a Few Words about Netiquette

Despite the decentralized nature of the Internet, certain standards have arisen that govern what people should and should not put into newsgroup messages. This loose, self-imposed code of behavior is referred to as *netiquette*. Basically, if you respect the following guidelines, you'll be a model newsgroup citizen:

- Don't try to sell anything. Newsgroups are supposed to be commercial-free zones.

- Don't use foul language. As a rule of thumb, don't write anything you wouldn't say in person to a group of people.
- Don't "flame" anyone. Flaming is the public, and often profane, criticism of another individual on the Internet.
- Don't propagate chain letters.
- Avoid "spamming." Spam in this case is not a lunch meat. Spamming means posting a lot of messages to a newsgroup on an irrelevant topic.
- It's possible to send messages to many newsgroups simultaneously. Don't cross-post messages to large numbers of newsgroups for which the messages aren't appropriate.

CAUTION

Another reason you should watch what you say is that your e-mail address is right at the top of every message you post, so everybody knows where to find you—at least in cyberspace.

Posting a New Message

Newsgroup messages take two forms: original messages with new subjects, and responses (also called follow-ups) to messages already posted. To post a new message, click Send New Message, which is available when you're viewing a newsgroup or an individual message.

EXPERT ADVICE

As a general rule, it's good to read a newsgroup for at least a week before jumping in with new posts. That's because topics you're interested in may already be part of an ongoing discussion, and you'll annoy other members if you clutter up the group with redundant questions.

STEP BY STEP Posting a Message

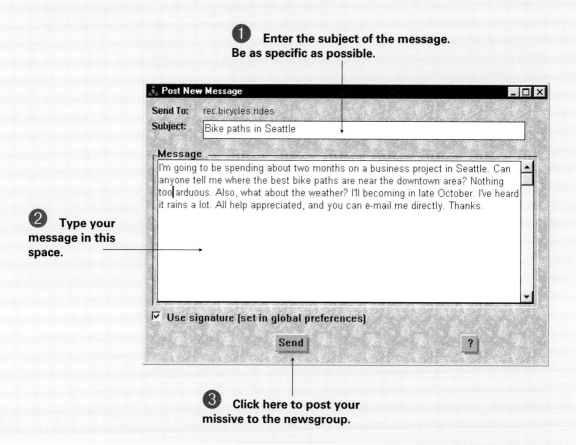

1 Enter the subject of the message. Be as specific as possible.

2 Type your message in this space.

3 Click here to post your missive to the newsgroup.

(Window: Post New Message)

Send To: rec.bicycles.rides
Subject: Bike paths in Seattle

Message

I'm going to be spending about two months on a business project in Seattle. Can anyone tell me where the best bike paths are near the downtown area? Nothing too arduous. Also, what about the weather? I'll becoming in late October. I've heard it rains a lot. All help appreciated, and you can e-mail me directly. Thanks.

☑ Use signature (set in global preferences)

Send

Sending a Response

There are two ways to respond to a message. You can reply only to the author of the message, by clicking E-mail to Author, or you can post a follow-up to the newsgroup as a whole by clicking Reply to Group, which generates the Post Response window, shown in Figure 5.7. This window contains two frames: one at the left containing the original message, and one at the right for your reply. If you want to include text from the original message in your reply, select it with your mouse and click Quote. After you finish composing your reply, click Send to post it to the newsgroup.

The subject appears here automatically.

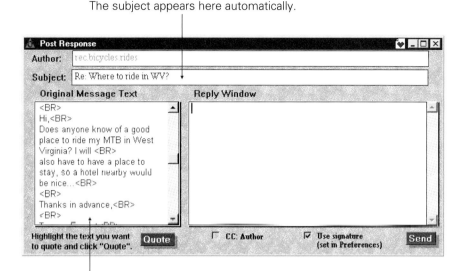

The text of the original
message appears here.

Figure 5.7 Use this window to respond to a message.

Wait a Minute—Cancel That!

Let's say you've fired off a newsgroup message and then immediately
regretted it. Perhaps you realize you have your facts wrong or you've inadvertently
insulted somebody. Believe it or not, it's possible to cancel the message. To do so,
you'll need the Message ID number, which appears beneath the date at the top of
the message. If you don't have that number, use the screen name you used to post
the message, the date the message was posted, and the name of the newsgroup to

EXPERT ADVICE

*If you want to send out some test messages, don't post them to bona fide
newsgroups. AOL has a newsgroup called aol.newsgroups.test specifically
for testing purposes. It's one of those groups that AOL automatically adds
to your list.*

which the message was sent. E-mail the information to the AOL screen name Newsmaster. AOL can cancel messages up to four days after they were posted.

Using Automatic AOL for Messages

The same Automatic AOL feature that you use to automatically retrieve e-mail (see Chapter 4) can also be used to fetch new newsgroup items so that you can read them when you're not connected to AOL. To use this feature, do the following:

1. Go to the main Newsgroups window and click Read Offline, which will display the dialog box shown in Figure 5.8.
2. Select each newsgroup you want to read offline and click Add to place it in the space at the right. Click Add All if you want to include all your groups. When you're finished, click OK.

Now all you have to do is set up Automatic AOL to retrieve the unread messages from the groups you've selected. To do that, choose Set up Automatic AOL from the Mail Center menu on the toolbar. The next time you run an Automatic AOL session, your new messages will be downloaded and stored in your Personal Filing Cabinet. To read them, just click My Files on the toolbar and choose Offline Newsgroups.

You can also compose responses to newsgroup messages while you're offline and use Automatic AOL to post them for you during an Automatic AOL session. Just click the appropriate option when setting up Automatic AOL.

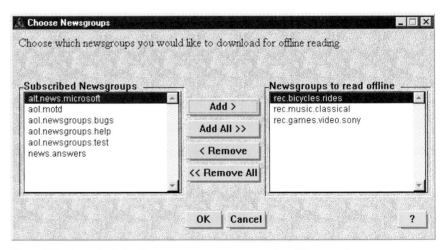

Figure 5.8 Use this dialog box to set up newsgroups for offline reading.

CAUTION

Automatic AOL downloads all unread messages in selected newsgroups to your PC. Before first using Automatic AOL, mark those groups as having been read. If you don't, you may end up with thousands of messages on your hard disk.

Customizing Your Newsgroup Experience

Some newsgroup features can be customized. Choose Set Preferences from the main Newsgroups window to display the dialog box shown in Figure 5.9, which contains several options:

- **Headers** If you want to see headers—the routing information that shows how a message traveled over the Internet—you can have them appear at the top or bottom of the message. But headers are essentially worthless. Do yourself a favor and stick with the default choice, which is to hide them.

- **Sort Order** You can change the order in which messages are displayed in your newsgroups' windows. Normally, the most recent messages are at the bottom of the list. If you'd rather have them at the top, choose Newest first.

- **Name style** If you'd like to have newsgroup names displayed in plain English rather than in their rec-comp-alt form, choose Descriptive Newsgroup Titles instead of Internet style names. For example, if you choose this option, the newsgroup rec.music.classical will be renamed as "Discussion about classical music." The only downside to this is that there are many newsgroups for which AOL doesn't provide common names. It's a hit-or-miss affair.

SHORTCUT

You can save newsgroups in your Favorite Places folder, thereby giving yourself ready access to them. Just drag the heart from the title bar of the Newsgroup window to the Favorite Places folder on the AOL toolbar.

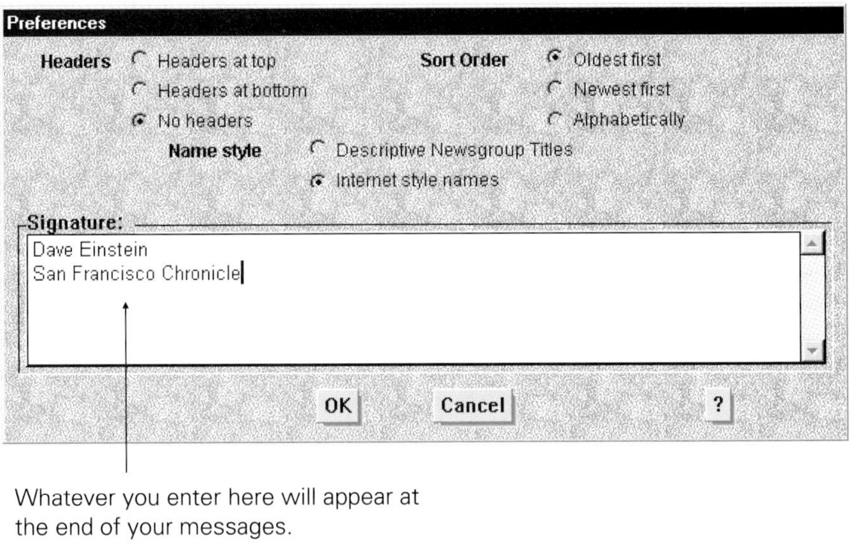

Whatever you enter here will appear at
the end of your messages.

Figure 5.9 Customize your newsgroup experience with the Preferences box.

Signing with a Flourish

The space at the bottom of the Preferences box is for a "signature" that you can automatically append to any newsgroup message you send. It's not your real signature—AOL isn't equipped to duplicate your handwriting—but it is a time-saving way for you to include information about yourself: your name, your nickname, or your company or organization name. But remember: newsgroup messages can be read by millions of people, so be frugal with sensitive personal information.

Limiting the Number of Messages

By default, AOL displays unread newsgroup messages for two weeks after they've been posted. If you discover that you have too many messages piling up, you can shorten this time limit for any newsgroup. This option is selected in a different Preferences dialog box. To invoke it, click Preferences in the window that displays the newsgroup you want to limit. At the bottom of the dialog box is a section, shown below, for setting the number of days, after which newsgroup items will be bounced.

Show messages no more than 14 days old.

Save   Cancel

Parental Controls

The best part about Parental Controls is that they're impossible to disable unless your kid knows your password and can sign on as you. (Only the person with the primary screen name can set Parental Controls.)

Because newsgroups reside on the Internet, they aren't subject to AOL's rules about language and behavior—so if you let your kids read any newsgroup they want, they're apt to run into subject matter that would make the devil himself blush. For example, it's possible to download sexually explicit photos from some newsgroups. The proliferation of controversial newsgroups has raised hackles in Congress, but so far the government hasn't figured out a way to clamp down on them without also clamping down on the First Amendment.

AOL, however, lets you block access to newsgroups that you think are too risqué for the younger set. Here's how:

1. Click Parental Controls in the main Newsgroups window.
2. Select the screen name of the child to whom the restrictions will apply.
3. Click Edit to display the Blocking Criteria dialog box, shown in Figure 5.10.

EXPERT ADVICE

Unless you block all newsgroups, it's impossible to guarantee a safe experience on the Internet, but you can eliminate many of the trouble spots by typing the letters alt *in the top space of the Blocking Criteria dialog box. Most pornographic newsgroups carry the alt designation.*

Other Internet Stuff on AOL

In addition to the World Wide Web and newsgroups, AOL provides access to other features that can help you find information on the Internet. These include FTP and Gopher, which you can access by going to the Internet Connection

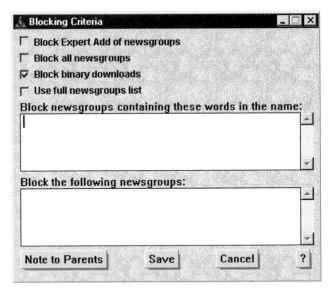

Figure 5.10 Use this dialog box to restrict newsgroup access for kids.

window and choosing Internet Extras. FTP and Gopher weren't exactly designed for busy people, but they're great if you really want to really dig into the vast storehouse of information on the Net. Here's what they do:

- **FTP** stands for *file transfer protocol.* This feature allows you to download files to your computer from libraries of files maintained by big institutions, especially universities. But using FTP to find files can be treacherous—and besides, many major FTP sites are now linked to the World Wide Web, which is a whole lot easier to use.

- **Gopher** is a system that uses menus to help you find information on the Internet. It was developed at the University of Minnesota and named after the school's mascot. Like FTP, it's a leftover from the days before the emergence of the Web, when you had to use arcane text commands to get anywhere on the Net. Using Gopher is a lot easier today, as you can see from the window shown in Figure 5.11.

Figure 5.11 Everything you ever wanted to know about Gopher

Now that we've pretty much covered the Internet, it's time to move on to the things that make AOL so special. In the next chapter, I'll start by showing you how to use message boards—the AOL equivalent to Internet newsgroups—and chat rooms, where you can hold live electronic conversations with other members on just about any topic that strikes your fancy.

Part 3

Making the Most
of Your Time Online

Message Boards and Chat Rooms—That's the Community Spirit!

- Using message boards
- Making the People Connection
- Finding your way around chat rooms
- Sending Instant Messages
- Attending big-time events on AOL Live

FAST FORWARD

Post a Message to a Message Board ➤ pp. 124-125

Sending a message to a message board is easy. Here's how:

1. Go to the message board you want (the channel windows provide access to most boards).
2. Click List All or List Unread to see a list of subjects.
3. Click Create Subject to open the Post New Message window.
4. Type the subject of your message and then the message itself in the spaces provided.
5. Click Send to post it to the message board.

Visit a People Connection Chat Room ➤ pp. 126-131

Want to visit with other AOL members and exchange opinions in real time? No problem. Just do the following:

1. Click People on the toolbar and then choose People Connection.
2. Click Find a Chat and then double-click a category to display a list of chat rooms for that topic.
3. To enter a room on the list, double-click it or click Go Chat. If the room's full, you'll be given the option to go to one just like it.

Have a Private Conversation ➤ pp. 131-132

You can have a one-to-one chat with another member in a chat room using the Instant Message feature. Just follow these steps:

1. Double-click the person's name in the list at the right that shows who's in the room.
2. In the dialog box that appears, click Message.
3. Enter your message and click Send. If the other person is up for it, you can have a running private conversation.

Set Up a Buddy List ➤ pp. 133-134

By creating a Buddy List, you can quickly see whether friends are online. If they are, you can send them instant messages and maybe get together in a chat room. Use the following steps to set up this feature:

1. Click My AOL on the toolbar, then choose View Buddy List.
2. Click Create and follow the instructions, entering a name for your list and adding your buddies' screen names.
3. Click Save.

Take in a Live Event ➤ pp. 134-136

AOL features regularly scheduled live online events that let you interact with top sports figures, film stars, politicians, and other famous folks. To see what's happening, click People on the toolbar and then choose AOL Live. You'll be taken to the AOL Live window, where you can find schedules of events and enter the virtual auditoriums where the action is.

Control Family Access to Chat Rooms ➤ pp. 136-137

Some chat rooms deal with sensitive topics, and their language can get bawdy. To prevent youngsters from seeing what they shouldn't:

1. Choose Parental Controls from the My AOL menu.
2. Choose Fine Tune with Custom Controls. If your child doesn't have a screen name, you must create one at this point. You can't impose restrictions without it.
3. Click Chat and then Chat Controls. Then choose the options you want.

America Online is often called a virtual community, and with good reason. Each day, thousands of its members exchange ideas, questions, answers, and opinions online. In fact, AOL may be the most vibrant community on the planet. It sure beats the town I live in, where the city council meets once a month and very few people even care. Anyway, this chapter is about the tools that let you get in on the action—AOL's message boards and chat rooms. If there's a hot topic—or even one that's not so hot—there's probably a message group or chat room devoted to it.

Different Ways to Communicate

Both message boards and chat rooms let you communicate directly with other AOL members. Message boards are electronic bulletin boards where you can post messages for others to read and read messages others have posted. Chat rooms offer more immediate gratification, giving you the opportunity to join in a live discussion using short messages that are displayed along with remarks by other members in a running dialog.

Finding Message Boards and Chat Rooms

AOL's channels provide access to message boards and chat rooms. In many cases, you can get to them simply by clicking a button in the channel window. For instance, there's the Grandstand button in the Sports channel, the Word of Mouth button in the Entertainment channel, and the Communities button in the

Lifestyles channel. In the Travel channel you just click Messages & Chat, which takes you to the window shown in Figure 6.1.

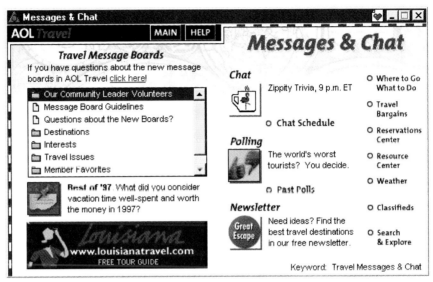

Figure 6.1   Your gateway to message boards and chat rooms about Travel

Message Boards

AOL's message boards are similar to Internet newsgroups. The difference is that participation in them is limited to AOL members. There are many more Internet newsgroups than message boards, but AOL message boards offer advantages that newsgroups don't: AOL's boards are often associated with other resources on the same topic, including chat rooms, news, and information.

DEFINITIONS

Post: *An item sent to a message board.*

Message: *An item sent to a message board.*

Confusion: *The result of having to deal with more than one word that means the same thing.*

How Message Boards Are Organized

Message boards can contain thousands of postings on dozens of topics. To keep things organized, message boards place messages in topic folders, like the one shown in Figure 6.2 for travel destinations in the Caribbean.

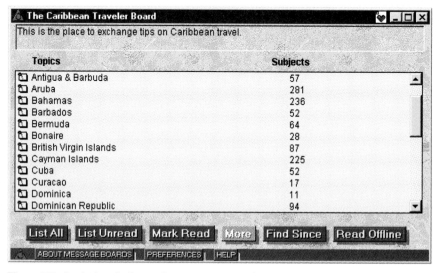

Figure 6.2 A window listing topics on a message board

Notice that along the bottom is a row of buttons. Here's what they do:

- **List All**   Displays a window listing subjects within a topic, and the number of messages for each subject. It includes all messages, regardless of whether you've read them.

- **List Unread**   Displays the same window as List All, but omits messages you've already perused. (If you double-click the name of the topic, it's the same as clicking List Unread.)

- **Mark Read**   Identifies all the messages in the topic as having been read. This is a useful button because it lets you virtually throw away old messages.

- **Find Since**   Displays a dialog box that lets you view stuff that's been posted recently or within a certain period of time.

- **Read Offline** Marks a topic so that its messages can be downloaded automatically using Automatic AOL. You can view a list of topics designated for offline reading by using the keyword **my boards**.

CAUTION

If you mark a topic for offline reading, you could end up with hundreds of messages on your hard disk if you aren't careful. To avoid that risk, click Preferences at the bottom of any message board window and set a limit on downloads.

Reading a Message

If you double-click one of the topics in Figure 6.2, you'll see a list of subjects within the topic. Some subjects have only one message, while others may have many—and some subjects are preceded by Re:, indicating that they contain responses to an earlier subject. To read the first message in a subject, select it and click Read Post at the bottom of the window (or just double-click the message in the list). Figure 6.3 shows a typical message, including information at the top about when it was sent and who sent it. (I've blacked out the sender's name to protect his privacy.)

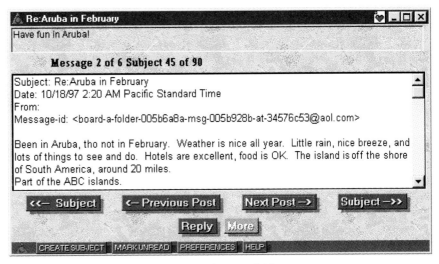

Figure 6.3 Sounds like Aruba is a great place to visit!

Okay, Now It's Your Turn!

If you came to the message board seeking information, answers, or opinions—which many busy people do—first scroll through the messages already there to see if perchance your issue has been addressed. If it hasn't, it's time to brush off your writing skills. Start by clicking Create Subject in the window for the topic upon which you wish to pontificate (you can also click Create Subject at the bottom of a window containing a message). Then follow the step-by-step instructions presented here.

STEP BY STEP Posting a New Message

① **Enter a few words describing your subject.**

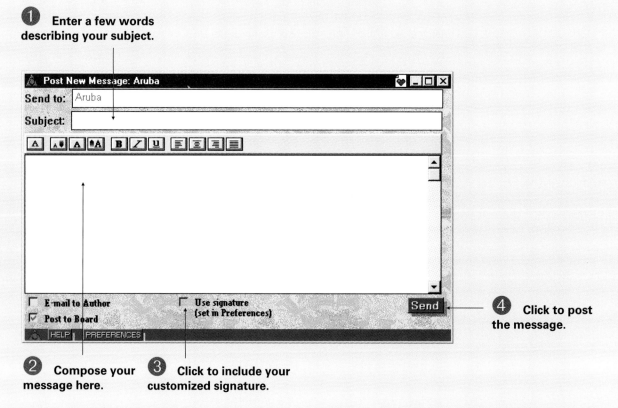

② **Compose your message here.**

③ **Click to include your customized signature.**

④ **Click to post the message.**

How to Make Your Prose Colorful

You don't have to be a poet to make a big impression with your writing. Just use the toolbar above the writing space in the Post New Message window to dress up your message. You can change the size of the type, or boldface, italicize, or underline it—even color it.

EXPERT ADVICE

Message board etiquette is roughly the same as for Internet newsgroups. Basically, be on your best behavior and refrain from posting any chain letters, commercial offers, or solicitations for pyramid schemes. And watch your language.

Add Your John Hancock to a Message   Your response will carry your AOL screen name, but you can also add an elaborate signature to your messages, offering information such as your real name and how people can reach you in the real world. To do that, click Preferences at the bottom of any message board window and create your signature in the space provided. You can even use different type sizes and colors. Then, each time you send a message, check the Use Signature box in the Post New Message window.

Responding to a Message

To reply to a message someone else has posted, click Reply at the bottom of the window displaying the message. This will bring up the Post Response window, which works just like the Post New Message window, with a couple of minor differences:

- The screen name of the person who sent the message to which you're replying is automatically entered at the top of the window.
- The subject is also filled in for you, with a Re: preceding it.
- You'll have the option of sending your reply by e-mail to the author of the original message. You can do this instead of posting it to the message board, or you can post it to the board and also reply personally to the author. It's your choice.

How About a Nice Chat

Message boards are a great way to share thoughts, questions, and opinions with other members—but they're not the only way. You can also engage in real-time discussions using Chat Rooms—online meeting places that happen to be the most popular feature on AOL. Thousands upon thousands of people each day participate in chat rooms, which are sprinkled throughout the service. For example, you can discuss sports trivia in a chat room in the Sports channel or debate the stock market in a Personal Finance chat room. The best way to introduce yourself to chat rooms is through the People Connection, which is devoted exclusively to helping you meet other members chatting online. To get there, just click the People button on the toolbar and choose People Connection. You'll see the window shown in Figure 6.4, which contains four main choices:

- **Show Me How**   Provides an online guide that will familiarize you with how chat rooms work.
- **The Community Center**   Offers information about AOL volunteers who host many chat room discussions, as well as tips on how to chat wisely and safely.
- **Find a Chat**   Lets you quickly locate a chat room on almost any topic you can think of.
- **Chat Now**   Takes you directly to a "lobby," where you can begin chatting immediately if you just can't wait to start. Lobbies are not dedicated to a particular topic.

EXPERT ADVICE

If you think a friend might also be online and chatting, it's easy to find him or her. Click People on the toolbar and choose Locate AOL Member, or just press CTRL-L. Then enter the person's screen name and click OK. If the person is in a chat room, this will track 'em down.

Figure 6.4 The main People Connection window

Finding a Chat

Let's start by going to Find a Chat, shown in Figure 6.5. You can get there either by clicking Find a Chat in the People Connection window or by choosing Find a Chat from the People menu on the toolbar. On the left side of the Find a Chat window you'll see a list of categories. Select a category and click View (or just double-click the category) to see a list of chat rooms in that category. To the left of each room is the number of members currently occupying it. Each room can hold up to 23 members. You can go to any room that isn't full by selecting it and clicking Go Chat, or simply by double-clicking the room in the list. If the room is full, you'll be given the option to go to one just like it.

Different Kinds of Chats

By default, the rooms displayed in Find a Chat are "featured chats"—that is, rooms that are open 24 hours a day and available to anyone who wants to come in. There are also two other kinds of rooms:

- **Member chats**   These are rooms created and named by members. Like featured chats, they are listed and open to anyone, but the

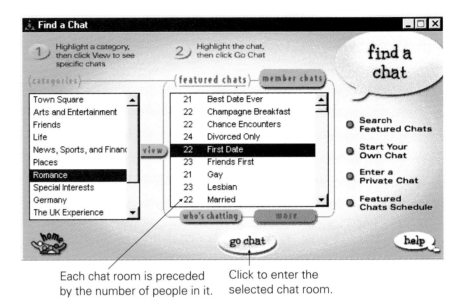

Each chat room is preceded   Click to enter the
by the number of people in it.   selected chat room.

Figure 6.5 It's easy to find the chat room you want.

subjects they cover are usually more specific—and can be rather controversial. To display a list of Member chats for a specific category, click Member Chats above the list of rooms and then pick a category on the left.

- **Private chats** These also are created by members. They are considered private because their names don't appear on any list. To enter a Private chat room, you have to know its name.

To create your own Member or Private chat room, click Start Your Own Chat in the Find a Chat window, or click People on the toolbar and choose Start Your Own Chat. This method can also be used to enter a Private chat, although there is also a separate button for that in the Find a Chat window.

Enough Talking—Let's Start Chatting!

For the sake of this discussion, let's start chatting by clicking Chat Now in the Find a Chat window or by choosing Chat Now from the People menu on the toolbar. As I mentioned, this takes you to a lobby in what is known as Town Square, even though it is neither in a town nor square. There can be hundreds of

EXPERT ADVICE

Private chats can be great for conducting long-distance conferences without relying on telephones. Just give all participants the name of the room and get them to enter it at a specified time, and chat your hearts out.

lobbies in Town Square with chats going on in them simultaneously—in Figure 6.6 I landed in Lobby 25. Fortunately, the lobbies all look the same.

Messages to a chat room appear in the order in which they are received by AOL's computers. If there are a lot of people in a room and more than one subject is under discussion, the on-screen conversation can look quite disjointed.

Chat Room Basics

In fact, all People Connection chat room windows share a common look and feel. There's a box at the right showing a list of members who are in the room. Comments from members appear on the screen as they enter AOL's computer system, and when the screen fills up, it automatically scrolls down to show the latest dialogue. If you want to participate, type your remarks in the space at the

Double-click a screen name to send the person an instant message.

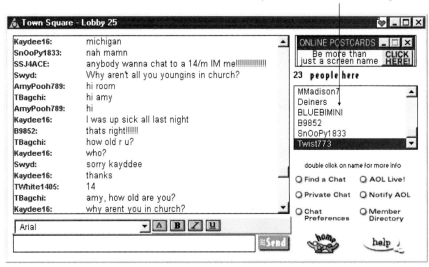

Figure 6.6 Lobbies are just chat rooms on no particular topic.

bottom of the window and then click Send. Your comments will appear just like everyone else's—unless you use the text formatting bar to change its size and color. But in practice, very few people do that, perhaps because it takes too long, and by the time you get the text the way you want it, the conversation has changed to a different subject.

Online Shorthand

Experienced chatters often use a computer-age version of shorthand to convey thoughts and emotions with a minimum amount of typing. You may not ever want to do this yourself—it is pretty nerdy—but it can save you time, and to a busy person that's always appealing. Here are some of the most common examples of online shorthand:

:)	smile
:D	smile/laugh/big grin
:*	kiss
;)	wink
:X	"my lips are sealed"
:P	sticking out tongue
{}	hug
:(	frown
:'(	crying
O:)	angel
}:>	devil
LOL	Laughing Out Loud
ROTF	Rolling on the Floor (laughing)
AFK	Away from Keyboard
BAK	Back at Keyboard
BRB	Be Right Back
TTFN	Ta-Ta for Now!

Want to see something cute? Turn this page 90 degrees clockwise and look at the shorthand symbols. Many of them actually look like what they represent. The smile symbol, for instance, looks like a person smiling.

WB	Welcome Back
GMTA	Great Minds Think Alike
BTW	By the Way
IMHO	In My Humble Opinion
WTG	Way to Go!

Chatting One-on-One with Instant Messages

In addition to chatting in public, as it were, you can have private conversations with other members in a chat room by using AOL's Instant Message feature. To do so, use the following steps:

1. In the list of participants on the right side of a chat window, double-click the name of the person for whom your message is intended.
2. In the dialog box that appears, click Send Message to display the Send Instant Message window.
3. The screen name of the recipient is automatically entered. Type your message in the space provided for it, as shown in the example here. Finally, click Send.

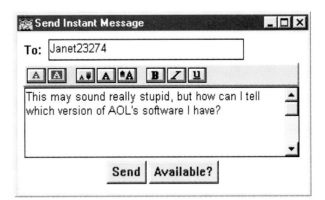

The message will appear instantaneously (that's why they call them Instant Messages) on the screen of the person at the other end. If that person replies to your message, the response will appear on your screen looking like this:

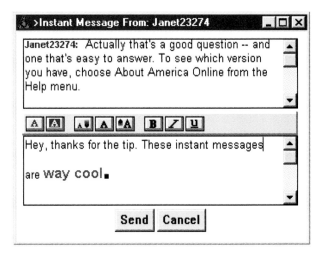

You can continue the conversation by using the Respond button. Each time a new reply is sent, it will be added to the window, giving you a running record of the conversation.

SHORTCUT

You don't have to be in a chat room to send an Instant Message, as long as both you and the recipient are online. Just click People on the toolbar and then choose Instant Message. To make sure your recipient is online, enter his or her screen name and click the Available? button.

AOL members can also use instant messaging to exchange online messages across the Internet with non-AOL members. The person on the other end must have the latest version of Netscape Communications' browser, which has AOL's Instant Message feature built-in.

Getting Rid of Distracting Chatter

Occasionally you'll encounter someone in a chat room who insists on ruining the experience for everyone else, with four-letter words, insults, or perhaps distracting sounds. No problem. Just double-click the person's name in the list of chat room participants and then check Ignore Member. That person's comments will no longer show up on your screen. Boy, don't you wish you could do that during some corporate meetings?

CAUTION

Unscrupulous members sometimes use Instant Messages to pretend they are AOL officials and request your password. If this happens while you're in a People Connection chat room, click the Notify AOL button and report the incident.

Keeping Track of Your Friends

There are probably times when one or more of your friends are online at the same time you are. Why not set things up so that AOL automatically notifies you with a beep each time one of your buddies signs on? That way you can exchange Instant Messages and maybe get together in a chat room. All you have to do is create a Buddy List Group, using the following steps:

You can have up to ten Buddy Lists per screen name, and each list can have as many entries as you want—with a maximum total of 10,050 names for all your lists. But that should be enough. I don't know anyone with 10,050 close buddies.

1. Choose Buddy List from the My AOL menu to display the dialog box shown in Figure 6.7.
2. Click Create and follow the instructions, entering a name for your list and adding your buddies' screen names to it.
3. Click Save.

Groups of buddies appear like this.

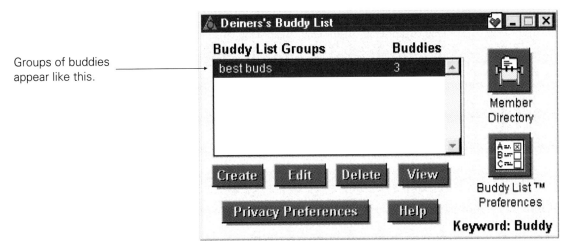

Figure 6.7 Use this box to create a Buddy List.

Once you've created a Buddy List, you can quickly check to see if anyone on it is online by choosing View Buddy List from the People menu. In addition, your computer will play a sound each time a buddy signs on or off. (If you don't like that idea, turn off the sounds using the Buddy List Preferences, which you can access from the dialog box shown in Figure 6.7.)

Live Events Online

Online events offer advantages over the real-life kind. You don't have to drive to get there, you don't have to pay to park, they're never sold out, and you can see perfectly from anywhere. Also, you never have to hunt for a restroom.

Regular chat rooms are great for small gatherings, but they're woefully inadequate for staging large events, such as question-and-answer sessions with movie stars, professional athletes, famous business people, and national politicians. For that, the place to turn is AOL Live, which features auditoriums capable of holding thousands of people. Click People on the toolbar and then choose AOL Live to go to the AOL Live window, shown in Figure 6.8.

Figure 6.8 The main window for AOL Live

It's Just Like Being There

Auditoriums differ from regular chat rooms in several ways. In the first place, you're in a virtual row with as many as 16 other members. Also, there's a virtual stage for the featured speaker or speakers along with a master of ceremonies. Figure 6.9 shows an example of an event in progress—in this case, a discussion with Carmen Electra, co-host of MTV's "Singled Out," and star of "Baywatch."

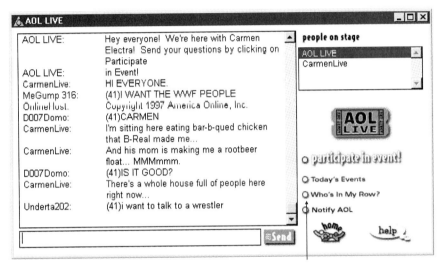

Click to see who's in your row or to move to another one.

Figure 6.9 A live event as it unfolds

How to Take Part in a Live Event

When you're in an auditorium, you can interact with the proceedings in two ways:

- Send a message to other members in your row by typing it in the space at the bottom of the window and clicking Send. (You won't see comments from people in other rows).

- Submit a question or comment to the speaker or speakers by clicking Participate in Event. This will bring up a dialog box in which you can enter your two cents' worth.

Finding Out Who's in Your Row, and Who's Moving

To see who's in your row with you, click Who's in My Row? in the auditorium window. This will display the window shown in Figure 6.10. You can send an instant message to anyone in the row simply by selecting the person's name and clicking Send Message. If you don't like the row you're in, click Other Rows. Then you can find out who's in any other row, and if it has fewer than 16 people in it, you can move there.

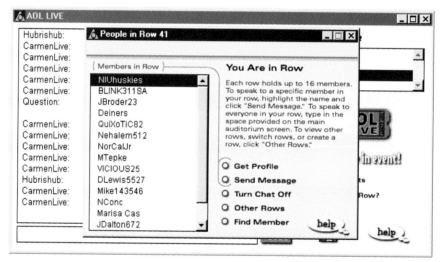

Figure 6.10 You can change rows or send a message to an individual in your row.

EXPERT ADVICE

If a featured speaker is really entertaining, you don't have to put up with chatter from other members. Click Who's in My Row and then click Turn Chat Off. Then you'll see only the questions and answers.

Recording Live Events
and Chats for Later Viewing

Chat sessions can progress quickly, with text scrolling on your screen at a rate that can make the online conversation hard to follow. If you're really looking forward to a big event on AOL Live, why not record the whole thing so you can view it again at your leisure after you've signed off? It's easy to do. Just use AOL's logging feature, which lets you capture incoming text in a file on your hard disk. Choose Log Manager from the My Files menu on the toolbar to bring up the Logging dialog box shown in Figure. 6.11. It provides two options: Chat Log and Session Log. The Chat Log is for recording chat transcripts. It works for any chat room or auditorium. The Session Log is for recording incoming text such as news or reference articles, posts from message boards, and even instant messages.

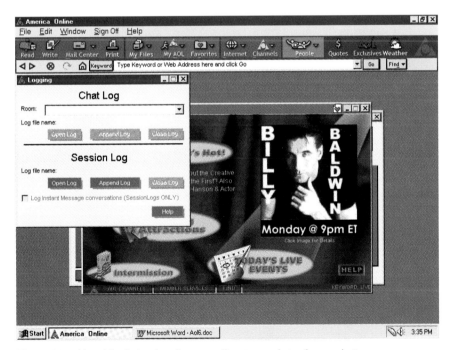

Figure 6.11 Use this dialog box for recording transcripts of your chats.

CAUTION

The Chat Log works only for chats and won't record other kinds of text. Similarly, the Session Log won't record a chat session. Make sure you pick the right option for what you want to do.

Ready, Set, Log!

To log a discussion, follow these steps:

1. Enter the chat room or auditorium where you'd like to log the discussion.
2. Open the Log Manager and click Open Log in the Chat Log section.
3. In the Open Log dialog box, note the destination folder and the name under which the log will be saved (you can change these if you like). Then click Save.
4. Go back to chatting. Actually, you can go elsewhere on AOL, too, and the chat will continue to be logged as long as the chat room window remains open.
5. When you want to stop logging, go to the Log Manager and click Close Log.

Viewing Something You've Logged   Logged chat transcripts are stored in plain text format. You can view the text either with any Windows-based word processor or with AOL itself. To use AOL, choose Open from the File menu. (You don't have to be signed on.) Locate the file in the Open a File dialog box that appears and click OK to view the file.

Controlling Access to Chat Rooms

Chat rooms can be like the Wild West. A lot of raucous and sometimes foul language gets tossed around, despite AOL's strict guidelines. If you have a young child who goes online without supervision, you might consider letting AOL act as a nanny by blocking access to some kinds of chat rooms. Here's how:

1. Click My AOL on the toolbar and choose Parental Controls.

Parental Control - Chat 4.0

Parental Control Chat

Block Chat All Rooms

Blocks access to all chat rooms on AOL.

Block Member Rooms

Blocks access to chat rooms created by other members on AOL.

Block Conference Rooms

Blocks access to the larger chat rooms throughout AOL.

Block Hyperlinks in Chat

Disables the use of hyperlinks in all chat rooms.

The screen names you have created are listed below. To restrict or block a screen name from using a feature, click on the appropriate box.

Screen Name	Block All Chat Rooms	Block Member Rooms	Block Conference Rooms	Block Hyperlinks in Chat
* Deiners	☐	☐	☐	☑
Einers	☐	☐	☐	☑
Dan1258928	☐	☐	☐	☑
Aaron20566	☐	☐	☐	☑

* Master screen name

[OK] [Cancel]

Figure 6.12 You can limit your kids' access to chat rooms

2. If your child doesn't have his or her own screen name, click Create a New Screen Name.

3. Choose Fine-tune with Custom Controls.

4. Click Chat and then Chat Controls.

5. Select the options you want on the screen shown in Figure 6.12. When you're done, click OK.

By the way, you can also use Parental Controls to prevent your child from sending or receiving Instant Messages.

CHECK POINT

As a service that you access on a computer, AOL could be expected to have a lot of resources for computer users—and boy, does it. In the next chapter, we'll take a look at some of them, including how to get free and inexpensive software while you're online.

CHAPTER

7

Everything You Ever Wanted to Know About Computers

INCLUDES

- Help for computer users

- Searching for software

- Downloading software

- Finding software on the Internet

- Connecting with companies

FAST FORWARD

Get Help with Computing Problems ➤ p. 144

Have a software question, or looking for a new modem? AOL can help. Just go to the Help Desk in the Computing channel. There you'll find tips on how to get the most out of Windows 95, a guide for new computer users, and access to chat rooms and message boards where you can get answers from other members.

Search for Software ➤ pp. 146-151

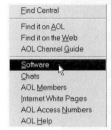

AOL offers more than 150,000 free and cheap software files that you can download to your PC. To find the files that meet your needs, use the Software Search feature:

1. Click Find on the toolbar and choose Software, then choose shareware.
2. Fill in the criteria, including the category and description of the software that interests you.
3. Click SEARCH to display a list of files that match your criteria.

Download a File ➤ pp. 152-153

When you find a file you want, you can transfer it from AOL's computer system to the hard drive on your PC by following these steps:

1. Click Read Description to see how large the file is and how long it will take to download.
2. Click Download Now to start the process. You will see the Download Manager dialog box that tells you the name of the file and the folder to which it will be downloaded. (By default files go to the Download folder in the AOL folder.) You might want to make a note of the filename and location.
3. Click Save to download the file.

View a Graphic ➤ pp. 154-155

You can use the AOL software to view and alter the appearance of many kinds of graphical images. You can even insert them into e-mail. Here's how to display an image:

1. Choose Open from the File menu. (You don't have to be signed on to do this. Just have the AOL software running.)
2. Use the dialog box that appears to locate the file.
3. Click Open to view the file.

Download More Than One File at a Time ➤ pp. 155-159

1. During an online session, select files to download, but click Download Later rather than Download Now. This will send the filenames to the Download Manager.
2. Before signing off, choose Download Manager from the My Files menu.
3. Click Download.
4. When the File Transfer dialog box appears, check the box labeled Sign Off After Transfer. When the last file has been transferred, you'll be automatically signed off.

Search the Internet for Software ➤ pp. 159-161

The World Wide Web is a great place to find software—and a good place to start searching through cyberspace is shareware.com. This site gives you access to some 200,000 software files located on computers around the world. Type **www.shareware.com** in the address box on the toolbar and press ENTER.

143

America Online is a service targeted at the personal computer, so it makes sense that it would cater to PC users—and that it does. The Computing channel offers information about personal computer companies, products, and trends, as well as a treasure trove of tips on how to get the most out of your PC. But AOL gives you more than just information. It gives you free or dirt-cheap software. That's right, actual software that you can install on your PC and run, without ever having to go to a store or load a disk. And that's not all—you also have access to hundreds of thousands of software files that reside on the Internet. Is that cool or what?

The Doctor Is In the House

Need some help with Windows 95? Looking for a good anti-virus program? Or maybe you're just perplexed by the new PC sitting in front of you. Fret not. The Computing channel, shown in Figure 7.1, is a veritable cornucopia of information, offering answers to most computer-related questions.

The first place to visit if you have questions about hardware or software is the Help Desk. Here you'll find such goodies as a New Computer User's Guide and areas that can help you become adept at using both AOL itself and the Internet. There are also chat rooms and message boards devoted to computing, where you can avail yourself of the expertise of other AOL members.

Figure 7.1 The Computing channel

The Smart Way to Shop

AOL's Computing channel features a Buyer's Guide that provides reviews of both hardware and software—and even lets you purchase many items online. Suppose you need a new monitor, but you aren't sure how to go about shopping for one. Click Buyer's Guide in the Computing channel and than choose Monitors, which will display the window shown in Figure 7.2. You can select from the list in the center to see reviews of major brand-name monitor models. By clicking the buttons at the left, you can also discover what to look for in a monitor and display a list of top-selling models.

In most cases, you can buy products online. When you click the picture of an item, you are instantly transported to the manufacturer's Web site, where you can make the purchase.

The AOL Computing Superstore

If you're one of those technophobes who still don't like the idea of putting their credit information on the Web, rest easy. A lot of computing stuff can be purchased through the Computing Superstore, which you can use with total peace of mind because AOL guarantees the security of your transaction. You can buy

The reviews in the Buyer's Guide are supplied by major magazines from Ziff-Davis and CMP, two leading publishers of computer magazines. The reviews are usually well-written and unbiased.

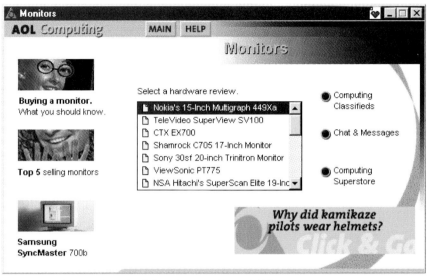

Figure 7.2 Who needs salesfolks when you have AOL?

laptop PCs and software, and some software can even be downloaded directly to your computer when you buy it. Is that convenient or what?

SHORTCUT

If you know what you're looking for, click Product Search in the Computing Superstore window. Then click Computing Superstore and type the name of the product. If it's available, you'll find out in a wink.

Cheap and Free Software

Not all software carries a big price tag. In fact, much of the best stuff is either free or dirt cheap. AOL makes available more than 150,000 such files, ranging from complete programs and games to graphical images. To access this treasure trove, click Download Software in the Computing channel, which displays the Download Software window. You'll find a list of broad topics, and double-clicking any topic folder will take you to a selection of categories within the topic, as shown in Figure 7.3.

Double-click a library
to view its files.

Figure 7.3 There's lots of shareware for desktop publishing.

Each day the folks at AOL pick a software file as the Daily Download. They're usually utilities or other small programs geared to helping make your life easier. One day recently, for instance, the Daily Download was a file for keeping track of numbers in a lottery.

There are three general categories of software that you can that you can download from AOL (or the Internet):

- **Shareware** These are programs that you can try out for free. If you like a piece of shareware, you're expected to pay for it. In almost every case, shareware is significantly less expensive than comparable programs in software stores—but just because it's less expensive doesn't mean it's inferior. Some of the best programs you can find are shareware.

- **Freeware** As the name implies, this is stuff that is available at no charge. Freeware generally consists of knickknacks such as clip art and simple file management utilities, but some excellent programs also fall into this gratis category.

- **Demoware** To entice customers, many software companies make demonstration versions of their programs available online so you can try them at no charge and decide whether they're worth buying. Basically, demoware is software from which some key features have been excluded, rendering the program less than fully functional. For instance, you might not be able to save files that you create using the demoware program.

DEFINITIONS

Download: To transfer data directly to your computer from another computer. You can download anything, from simple text to complex graphics, using a telephone line and a modem.

Upload: To transmit information from your computer to another computer (the opposite of download). You can even upload files to AOL for other members to use, although if you're a busy person, this thought probably will not occur to you.

Hunting for Software to Download

If you want to cut to the chase, use AOL's extensive searching capabilities to find exactly the kind of software you want. To start your search, do one of the following:

- Click Software Search in the Download Software window and then choose Shareware.
- Click Find on the toolbar and then choose Software, then choose Shareware.

Either way, you'll be transported to the Software Search dialog box, shown in Figure 7.4. Fill in the search criteria, click the Search button, and voilà! You'll see a list of files that you can download.

Check a category
or two to focus
the search.

Software Search

1. *Select a Timeframe:* *Choose only one*
   ⊙ All Dates   ○ Past Month   ○ Past Week

Today in the Superstore...
Computing Superstore

2. *Select a Category:* *Choose the categories you wish to search:*

☐ Applications   ☐ Games   ☐ OS/2
☐ Development   ☐ Graphics & Animation ☐ Telecommunications
☐ DOS   ☐ Hardware   ☑ Windows
☐ Education   ☐ Music & Sound

3. *Enter a Search Definition:* *Narrow search by typing in key words.*

| pictures of birds | **SEARCH** |

| COMPUTERS & SOFTWARE | MAC SEARCH | HELP | Keyword: FileSearch

Figure 7.4 Searching for software couldn't be easier

Narrowing the Hunt

To quickly track down exactly the software you want, use the right words
to focus your search. Suppose, for instance, that you're looking for pictures of cars
to add to a newsletter. Searching for the word *cars* produces 2,231 possibilities,
which is far more than you, as a busy person, have time to sort through. So try
narrowing the hunt. Searching for the phrase *car art* produces 125 files. Putting
the kind of car in the search really cuts it down. I tried searching just for *ferrari*
and was rewarded with 14 matches, including the one shown in Figure 7.5.

EXPERT ADVICE

*To locate free files, include "distribute freely" in your search phrase. This
will find files that you can use without incurring a fee. Similarly, if you're
looking just for shareware files, include "shareware" in your search
phrase.*

Figure 7.5 Nice full-color shot of a Ferrari racing car

Boy, This Thing Works Fast!

When you conduct a search, AOL's heavy-duty database search engine proceeds to ferret out the files that match your search criteria. The process takes just a few seconds, after which the files are listed in the File Search Results window, as shown in Figure 7.6. In this search, I was looking for Acrobat Reader. Acrobat Reader lets you view files that have been formatted with Adobe's Acrobat technol-

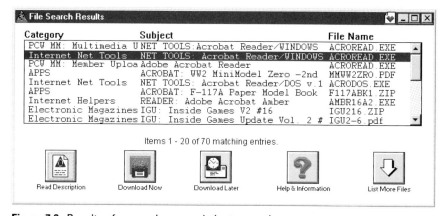

Figure 7.6 Results of a search appear in just seconds.

ogy, which makes documents appear online exactly as they do in print. Many companies and government agencies now use Acrobat to publish such documents as annual reports and tax forms on the Internet.

Checking Out the Particulars

When you select a file and click Read Description at the bottom of the window, you'll be able to view some germane facts about the file before you commit to downloading it. For example, you can see how large the file is (for Acrobat Reader, a hefty 1,528,560 bytes) as well as the approximate time it will take to download (14 minutes with a 28.8 kbps modem). You'll also get a brief description of the file, including instructions on how to install and use it once it's been downloaded.

Need More Assistance? No Problem!

If you want more information about downloading, click Ask the Staff at the bottom of the window that shows the description of a file. That will take you to the Download Info Center, where you'll find the answer to almost any question about downloading.

Thank Goodness for File Compression

Large programs involve several files, which would take forever to download separately. But it's possible to pack many files into one file and shrink the file down to a manageable size. This is called file compression. Most compressed files that can be downloaded end in either .exe or .zip. Files ending in .exe are usually compressed programs. Files ending in .zip can be either programs or collections of files.

DEFINITIONS

.exe: The file extension of an executable file. A compressed file ending in .exe is a self-extracting file. Running the file automatically extracts any files within it and restores them to normal size.

.zip: The file extension of a file compressed with a zip utility. Files with this extension must be decompressed with an unzip utility. AOL automatically unzips zipped files when you sign off after downloading.

Downloading

If you decide to download a file, you can do so either from the file's description window or from the File Search Results window. In either case, click Download Now to display the Dialog Manager dialog box.

STEP BY STEP Downloading a File

1 Select the folder where the file will be stored.

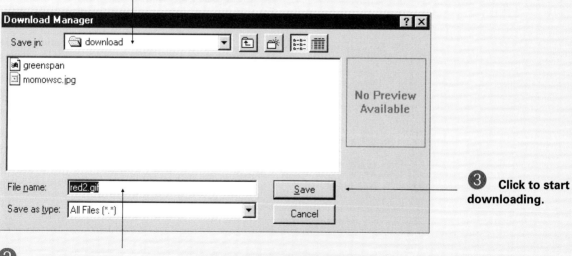

3 Click to start downloading.

2 Verify or change the name of the file you're getting.

CAUTION

You can change the name of a file to be downloaded, but don't mess with the last three letters that follow the period. If you alter the extension of a program file, compressed file, or graphics file, the file won't work.

Ready, Set, Transfer!

When you're satisfied with the information in the dialog box and click Save to start the download, you'll see a File Transfer dialog box (see Figure 7.7) that shows you the progress of the download, lets you know approximately how much more time the transfer will take, and gives you the option of canceling the operation or pausing and finishing it later.

Clicking here stops the download, but you can resume it later.

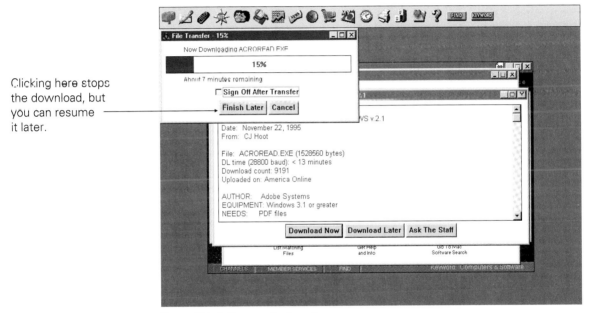

Figure 7.7 A file transfer in action

Okay, It's Been Downloaded—Now What?

Installing and using programs that you have downloaded is fairly simple. Here's how to go about it:

1. Using the Windows Explorer, the Windows 95 file management system, locate the file in the AOL Download folder.
2. If the filename ends in .exe, double-click it to start the installation process. If the original file was a .zip file that AOL has automatically unzipped, the program will have been put into a folder of its own

within the Download folder. Open that folder and double-click the installation file, which is usually named setup.exe or install.exe.

Graphics, Sounds, and Videos

You can download pictures and audio and video files—then view or listen to them using AOL's own built-in capabilities. AOL can't decode all the different multimedia formats, but it handles most of the major ones, including GIF, JPEG, and bitmap (.bmp) graphics files (but not TIFF and WMF files). AOL also lets you view AVI movie clips and listen to WAV sound files. To open any of these files, you don't have to be online (but you can be). Just make sure your AOL software is running and then follow these steps:

1. Choose Open from the File menu.
2. Use the dialog box that appears to locate the file you want.
3. Click OK to view the file. Here's a graphic showing me working on this book:

Highly confused

Don't Like the Way an Image Looks? Change It! When you open certain kinds of graphics files in AOL, you'll notice a row of buttons across the top of the window. These let you change the way the image appears. You can rotate it, flip it from right to left or upside down, and heighten or reduce the brightness

DEFINITIONS

GIF: Graphics interchange format; a method of compressing graphical images. GIF files use the extension .gif.

JPEG: Joint Photographic Experts Group format, a technique that provides better compression than GIF. JPEG is used mostly for complex artwork and photos. The file extension is .jpg.

Bitmap: A Windows-compatible format whose files are called bitmapped graphics. The file extension is .bmp. (Microsoft uses .bmp files for the wallpaper in Windows.)

TIFF: Tagged Image File Format, a standard format for scanned images. The file extension is .tif.

WMF: Windows Metafile Format. The file extension is .wmf.

AVI: Audio Video Interleaved. This is a video format for Windows developed by Microsoft.

WAV: A Windows sound file. Watch out; they take up lots of disk space.

and contrast. A button at the bottom of the window lets you insert the image into an e-mail message form.

One Example of a Great Shareware Program

If you plan to use a lot of clip art and other images, you may need a program with better graphics-handling abilities than AOL. It just so happens that you can download such a program. It's called Paint Shop Pro (see Figure 7.8). It's shareware, and it's better than just about any comparable program on the market. To find it, click the File Search button on the toolbar, select the Windows category, type **Paint Shop Pro**, and press ENTER.

Using the Download Manager

Let's say you want to download one or more files, but you don't really have the time to do it. Perhaps you have a big report to get out of the way, and you need to use AOL for some research. No problem. Instead of clicking Download

Figure 7.8 Paint Shop Pro is shareware at its best.

Now after you locate the file you want, click Download Later. This will add the name of the file to AOL's Download Manager. You can queue up as many files as you want in this manner. Then, when you're ready to sign off, do the following:

1. Choose Download Manager from the My Files menu. You'll see a window listing the files you've chosen, as in Figure 7.9.
2. Click the Download button.
3. When the File Transfer dialog box appears, select Sign Off After Transfer.

From that point on, AOL takes over. The files you've listed will be downloaded, and when the last one has been transferred, AOL will sign you off. How's that for convenience?

EXPERT ADVICE

You can use Automatic AOL to download files listed in the Download Manager during off-peak hours. Just set Automatic AOL to run at a specific time and make sure you've checked the Download Selected Files box.

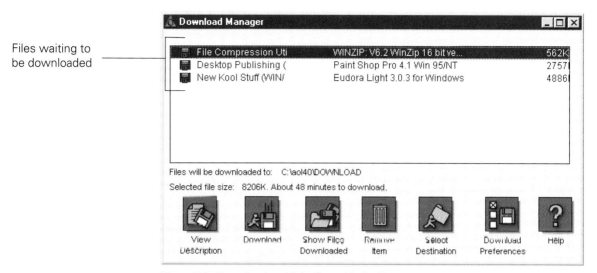

Files waiting to be downloaded

Figure 7.9 Download multiple files with the Download Manager.

Keeping Track of Files You've Downloaded

AOL keeps track of your downloads. To see a list of the files you have downloaded, choose Download Manager from AOL's My Files menu and then click Show Files Downloaded. This will display the Files You've Downloaded window, which looks like the Download Manager window but has some different buttons at the bottom. One of them, Show Status, displays a File Information box:

This box shows the name of a selected file and tells you where it is on your hard drive (just in case you put it somewhere other than the default folder and can't find it).

Downloadus Interruptus, or Finishing Later

At any time while you're performing a download, you can pause the process without losing the time you've already invested. Say, for example, that you're halfway through a 30-minute download and you remember that you're supposed to pick up your son after soccer practice. Like right now. Don't panic. Just click Finish Later in the File Transfer dialog box. The portion of the file that has already been transferred will be stored on your hard drive, and the file will be listed in the Download Manager. You can resume the download at any time by selecting the file in the Download Manager and clicking Start Download.

State Your Preferences

The Download Manager window also includes a button that lets you set download preferences. Press the button, and here's what you'll see:

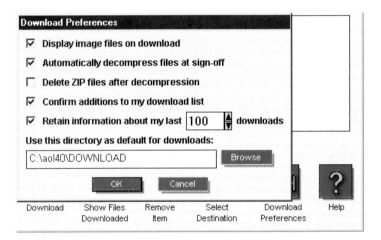

This box offers you several options. Here are descriptions of the most useful ones:

- **Display image files on download** AOL can display images on the screen while they're being downloaded. (This works only if you're downloading an image from AOL's software libraries. It doesn't work for images you get from the Internet.) This option is useful because it lets you evaluate an image as it's coming in. You can then decide to cancel the download if the picture is a dog (unless, of course, you're downloading a picture of a dog).

- **Automatically decompress files at sign-off** When you sign off, AOL will automatically decompress zipped files if you have selected this option. An alternative is to select the file in the Files You've Downloaded window and click the Decompress button.

- **Delete ZIP files after decompression** You can have AOL delete zipped files after it decompresses them. This is safe to do because after the files have been extracted, you'll no longer need the zipped file itself. However, it's not a bad idea to keep the zipped file at least long enough to save it on a floppy disk (if it will fit). That way you'll have it if you ever need it again.

The Internet—A Software Clearinghouse

AOL's enormous repository of files is impressive, but it's nothing compared to the wealth of software that resides on the Internet. Major universities, corporations, and other large organizations maintain huge libraries of freeware, shareware, and demoware. Much of it duplicates the software found on AOL, but there's also a lot of esoteric, rare stuff on the Web that you can't find anywhere else.

CAUTION

Computer viruses can infect your PC without your knowing it. They can arrive in e-mail messages or in files that you download from the Web. The best way to protect yourself is to equip your computer with a good anti-virus program. AOL makes one such program, Dr. Solomon's Anti-Virus, available for a free trial. Use the keyword virus info *to get it.*

Searching the Web for Software

A good place to start your cyber-search is shareware.com, shown in Figure 7.10. To get there, type **www.shareware.com** in the address space on the toolbar and press ENTER. This site, operated by CNET, is an all-encompassing online clearinghouse for shareware and freeware. It boasts access to some 200,000 files in various locations around the world. You use these sites much as you do AOL's own File Search feature: enter a word or phrase describing the file you'd like to find and then let the search engine do its stuff.

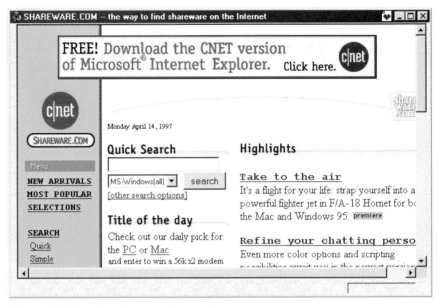

Figure 7.10   There's software aplenty at shareware.com.

Downloading from the Web

You download files from the Internet in basically the same way that you download files from AOL. When you find a file you want to download, you click the hypertext link to start the downloading process. A Save As dialog box appears, with the name of the file already entered and the AOL Download folder designated as the default destination. Click OK to start the download.

Now for the Bad News...

Although the Web offers a wealth of software, there are some distinct advantages to using AOL's libraries whenever possible. These include:

- **Manageability** You can't use the Download Manager for Internet files.
- **Reliability** You can almost always get software from AOL without a hitch, whereas many Internet software libraries suffer from traffic jams that can keep you from even accessing sites.
- **Safety** AOL checks its own downloadable files for viruses. With the Internet, you're on your own.

EXPERT ADVICE

AOL does not automatically unzip zipped files that you download from the Internet. For that, you'll need a special program. But don't fret—a great shareware program called WinZip is available for downloading. Just go to the Software Search window and search for the word "Winzip."

ZDNet—Yet Another Option

As if you don't now have enough options for finding and downloading software, here's another one: ZDNet. This is an extensive area on AOL operated by Ziff-Davis, the computer-magazine publishing giant. The easiest way to access it is by using the keyword **ZDNet**. Once there, click the button labeled Download, which gives you access to the ZDNet software library, shown in Figure 7.11. (You can also get to this site directly on the Web with the address www.hotfiles.com.) Not only is this library extensive and well-organized, but Ziff-Davis also rates many software files, giving you a good idea of what's hot and what's not.

Figure 7.11 ZDNet offers yet another place to find software.

The Company Connection

SHORTCUT

You can reach most of the companies that have areas on AOL by using keywords. Just type the name of the company as the keyword.

One of the big advantages you'll get from using AOL is the ability to access technical support and advice from hundreds of computer and software companies. Anyone who has ever tried to use a big software company's telephone support line knows what a nightmare it can be. It's great to know that you can find answers right there on AOL. To view a list of companies by name or category, click Companies in the Computing channel. There you can also search for a company by name or product. Figure 7.12 shows the main window for Brøderbund, which sells the Carmen Sandiego series and Myst.

Figure 7.12 Computer-industry companies have their own areas on AOL.

If there's anything that AOL users want more than free software, it's news and information—and that leads us nicely into the next chapter, in which I'll show you how to expand your knowledge of the world any time, day or night (in case you have trouble sleeping).

8

News You Can Use and Other Stuff That's Good to Know

INCLUDES

- The latest headlines

- Slideshows

- Customizing your news

- Encyclopedias and dictionaries

- Finding people and places

- Help with homework

FAST FORWARD

Check Out the Latest Headlines ➤ pp. 168-170

Keep on top of the news with AOL's News channel, which you'll find in the main Channels window. By clicking This Hour's Headlines in the News channel, you can view a summary of the top stories of the world as they unfold. To view headlines for a specific news department, click the button for the department, such as Business, Sports, or Politics.

View a Multimedia Slideshow ➤ pp. 170-171

With AOL's slideshow feature, you can view multiple images of a news story while listening to an audio narrative. ABC News slideshows on breaking stories and important news events can be found in the News channel. You don't need any special software to watch a slideshow. Just sit back and enjoy the show.

Create a News Profile ➤ pp. 174-175

Set up a news profile so that AOL can deliver customized news to you every day via e-mail.

1. Click My AOL on the toolbar and choose News Profiles. Then click Create a Profile.
2. Give your profile a name and indicate the maximum number of stories you want each day, up to 50. Then click Next.
3. Enter search words to help AOL select only the news you want to see. There are three different kinds of criteria to enter. Click Next after finishing each one.
4. Choose the news sources you want searched and then click Next.
5. Click Done to activate the news profile.

Catch Up on Your Favorite Magazine ➤ *pp. 175-177*

The Newsstand department of the News channel features dozens of online versions of major magazines. In addition to giving you articles from the current issue, many magazines let you search back issues and download graphics.

Click image for BW Contents

Use an Encyclopedia Without Going to the Library ➤ *pp. 180-181*

AOL's Research & Learn channel features three encyclopedias: from Compton, Columbia, and Grolier. Just click Encyclopedia in the Research & Learn channel and choose the one you want. They're a lot better than printed encyclopedias because they don't take up shelf space, they're easy to search, and they don't go out of date.

Find People and Places ➤ *p. 183*

The Phone & Addresses button in the Research & Learn channel gives you access to online directories including white pages and yellow pages. These let you easily find people and places throughout the country, and they can save you money as well, because you won't have to pay the telephone company for directory assistance.

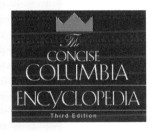

Phone & Addresses Resources

Stumped by Homework? Ask a Teacher ➤ *pp. 186-187*

AOL can help you or your child with those tough homework problems that nobody in the house can answer. Just do the following:

1. In the Research & Learn channel, select Ask-A-Teacher.
2. Choose the appropriate age group from three options: Elementary School, Jr. High and High School, and College and Beyond.
3. Get help by going to a tutorial chat room, e-mailing a teacher, posting a message to an academic message board, or delving into an extensive education database.

Ask-A-Teacher

▶ Elementary School

▶ Jr. High and High School

▶ College and Beyond

Keyword: Ask-A-Teacher

167

Online services began years ago by offering news and information. Today, that's still one of AOL's strongest features. You can read the latest news as it breaks and peruse online versions of newspapers, magazines, and broadcast services. In this chapter you'll examine the various ways to peruse world and national news using AOL's News channel as well as how to get news and other information about the area where you live using the Local channel. Then it's off to the Research & Learn channel to soak up knowledge from encyclopedias, dictionaries, and other sources. You'll also discover how to get help with school work, from elementary school through college. By the end of this chapter, you're definitely going to be in the know.

What's New in the News?

As the name implies, the News channel, shown in Figure 8.1, is where you'll find the latest developments in national and world news, along with sports, business, and weather. AOL gathers the news from a variety of sources, including the Associated Press, Reuters, ABC, and the *New York Times*. So let's go there first. Just click News in the Channels window.

The News channel is divided into departments, corresponding to the sections you might find in a daily newspaper—but it's much easier to use than a newspaper. Suppose, for instance, that you just want the top stories of the day. No

Figure 8.1 The News channel

problem. Just click This Hour's Headlines. A window will pop up that gives you a quick rundown of the latest breaking stories.

In-Depth News, AOL Style

On the right side of the News channel, you'll see a list of top stories. Click one to see the full scoop, plus links to related stories that can help put the news in perspective for you. As I'm writing this book, for example, the world is marking the fortieth anniversary of Sputnik, the first man-made satellite. As you can see in Figure 8.2, AOL offers all kinds of information, including a photo gallery and a timeline of the space race. It's the kind of in-depth treatment that AOL gives most big stories, and what sets AOL apart from other news.

SHORTCUT

If you know what you're looking for, you can probably find it by searching through AOL's news and information database. Just click Search & Explore in the News channel and follow the instructions.

Figure 8.2   Everything you ever wanted to know about Sputnik

Get the Big Picture with Slideshows

Slideshows aren't just for breaking news. AOL has a whole host of them on sports and entertainment topics as well. To view a list of available slideshows, use the keyword slideshow.

Online services and the Internet aren't quite ready for full-motion video. The problem is that your telephone line, through which you receive AOL, doesn't have the capacity to carry TV-quality images. But AOL offers the next best thing: multimedia slideshows. Throughout the News channel—and on other channels as well—you'll see links to slideshows on stories and events. Each show consists of a series of images that change all by themselves, accompanied by an audio narrative. It's pretty cool, and of course, it's free as part of your AOL service. Figure 8.3 shows you a slideshow about the death of singer John Denver.

How's the Weather Out There? With AOL, you never have an excuse for getting caught in the rain without an umbrella. By using the Weather department in the News channel—or simply clicking Weather on the toolbar—you can learn the up-to-the-minute weather conditions and forecast for almost any place in the world. Whether you're traveling to the coast on business or you just want to see how deep the snow is back in Vermont where your brother-in-law lives (ha-ha!), AOL can give you the scoop. You'll find local temperatures, maps, even satellite photos. Figure 8.4 shows a regional map of the northeastern United States. Looks like pretty good weather in New York tonight.

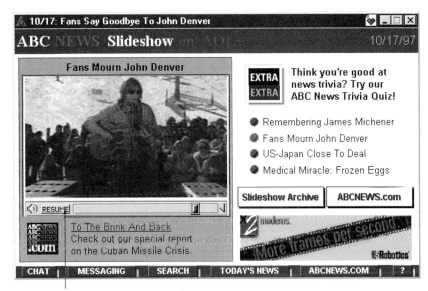

This button lets you pause and
resume the slideshow.

Figure 8.3 AOL's slideshows provide visual images and sound.

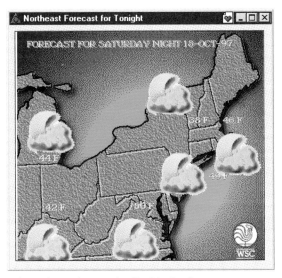

Figure 8.4 Guess I won't need my umbrella this time!

Checking Out the Local Scene

Sure, it's great to know what's going on in other parts of the world, but wouldn't it be cool to also have instant access to the news in your area? No problem. Just click the Local department in the News channel and then choose your city from the list. You'll be taken to a window that's brimming with the latest local news, like the one shown in Figure 8-5. This service is part of Digital City, which offers all kinds of information about most big metropolitan areas, including New York, San Francisco, Boston, and Washington, D.C. Digital City can be accessed by choosing AOL's Local channel. You'll learn more about the goodies offered by Digital City in Chapter 12.

Click here for local weather.

Click here to go to the main page of your digital city.

Figure 8.5 Catch up on local news with Digital City.

If You Like Something You Find, Keep It

Suppose you want to keep an article so you can refer to it later. No problem. AOL gives you several options, the easiest of which is simply to print it. With the

EXPERT ADVICE

AOL's news isn't the only game in town. Every major network and most big newspapers also have Internet sites. Especially good ones include USAToday (www.usatoday.com), MSNBC (msnbc.com), and for sports, ESPN (espn.com). All the big search engines, including Yahoo (www.yahoo.com) and Excite (www.excite.com), also offer breaking news, weather, and sports.

article on the screen, just choose Print from the File menu. This function acts like Print in any word processor. You don't have to worry about type fonts or anything else.

Saving an Article

You can save any text that's displayed on your screen, whether its from a news article, a magazine, or a reference source like an encyclopedia (we'll get to those later in this chapter). To save an article, or part of one, follow these steps:

1. With the article on the screen, select the text you want to save or choose Select All from the Edit menu. Then choose Copy from the Edit menu.
2. Choose New from the File menu to display an empty text window.
3. Choose Paste from the Edit menu.
4. Choose Save As from the File menu and give your story a name. Then click Save.

Next time you want to read the article, choose Open from the File menu and double-click the article's name

EXPERT ADVICE

Are you looking for something in particular in a news article, such as mention of a certain person or place? Here's how to find it: Choose Find in Top Window from the Edit menu and type the word or words you're looking for. Then click Find Next.

You can have up to five news profiles for every screen name on your account. That means you can customize one profile to get stories about your favorite baseball team, another to follow the presidential election, a third to grab news on companies whose stock you own. There are all kinds of possibilities.

Customized News Delivery

Sure, it's great to be able to scan headlines and search for the latest news, but wouldn't it be great if you could get stories about your favorite topics delivered directly to you every day? Say no more. AOL has created just such a service, called News Profiles. It delivers stories to you as e-mail, a convenient way to get your daily dose of customized news. The best part is there's no newspaper to toss at the end of the day. Just delete the stories you don't want and keep the ones you do.

Creating a News Profile

To take advantage of this nifty feature, you must set up one or more news profiles for yourself. Each profile generates specific kinds of news based on criteria that you set. To create a profile, click My AOL on the toolbar and then choose News Profiles. This will display the News Profiles dialog box:

Then, follow these steps:

1. Give your profile a name and indicate the maximum number of stories you want each day, up to 50. Then click Next.
2. Enter search terms to help AOL select only the news you want to see. There are three different kinds of criteria to enter. Click Next after finishing each one.
3. Choose the news sources that you want searched and then click Next.
4. Click Done to activate the news profile.

Once you've created a profile, you can modify it (or even get rid of it) any time you want. Just click Manage Your Profiles in the News Profiles dialog box.

CAUTION

Your AOL mailbox can hold only 550 pieces of mail—and that includes mail you've already read. If you have several news profiles active and they're each delivering up to 50 items each day, your mailbox could fill up fast. If the situation starts to get out of hand, reduce the limit on the number of articles that you get, or try more selective search terms.

The Newsstand

AOL makes available online versions of nearly 100 newspapers and magazines There are publications devoted to business and finance, computers, and science, not to mention sports, religion, music, and even the military. In many cases, you get photos and graphics along with text, and some publications even let you search through back issues. Several channels, including News, Computing, and Families, have their own Newsstand sections where you'll find publications related to the content in the channel.

Some publications in the Newsstand are also available on the World Wide Web. In many cases, however, the AOL versions are easier to use and offer more features, such as the ability to search for articles in previous issues.

All the News That's Fit to Print on Your Screen

For all you news hounds, the first place to stop is the online version of the *New York Times,* America's newspaper of record (see Figure 8.6). You'll find it by clicking the Newsstand department in the News channel. The *Times* was at one time so influential that each evening radio stations would read a list of what it was planning for the front page the next day. With AOL, you can go that one better by reading the stories themselves when you get up in the morning.

Figure 8.6 The AOL version of the *New York Times*

EXPERT ADVICE

Any article from a Newsstand publication can be printed, copied, or saved using the same procedures you used for news articles earlier in this chapter. This is a great resource for schoolwork and other research. Just remember that all proprietary material in AOL magazines and newspaper articles is protected by copyright law.

Getting Down to Business

One of the most comprehensive magazines available on AOL is *BusinessWeek Online* (see Figure 8.7), which is available in the News channel Newsstand. Here you'll find the complete text of the weekly magazine, along with photos, charts, and other graphics. In addition to the regular magazine, *BusinessWeek Online* offers a special service, BW Plus, which is chock-full of information aimed straight at busy people. There's a list of the top business schools, information on mutual funds, even a small business center.

Figure 8.7 *BusinessWeek* has an impressive area on AOL.

A Cornucopia for Consumers

One example of a magazine that really benefits from being online is *Consumer Reports*, which can be found in the Newsstand section of the Families channel. You can find information about products that have appeared in the magazine faster online than you can with the printed issues. You can search by subject, or you can quickly find reviews, test results, and ratings under topics such as Automobiles, Electronics, and Food & Health. Figure 8.8 shows the Automobile section, where you can easily learn what the folks at *Consumer Reports* think of your car.

Knowledge at Your Fingertips

Until just a few years ago, if you wanted access to extensive reference information, you had to go to the public library. AOL is like having a reference library inside your computer—only better. It's open 24 hours a day, 7 days a week, and you don't have to get in your car and drive to it, and best of all, you don't have to worry about overdue books. Just go to the Research & Learn channel, shown in Figure 8.9.

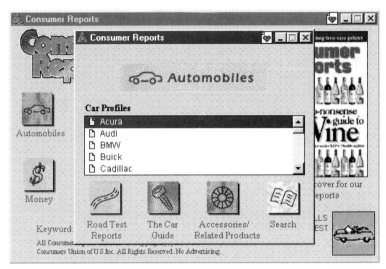

Figure 8.8 Check out *Consumer Reports* before buying a car.

Using this channel, you can access information on AOL and the Internet covering a wealth of topics, from history and geography to science and education. Clicking any subject will display a list of resources.

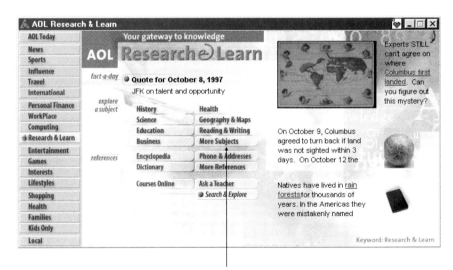

More Subjects includes art, jobs, money, and law.

Figure 8.9 The Research & Learn channel

Seek and Ye Shall Find

Like the News channel, Research & Learn lets you search for specific information. This can save you the trouble of poring through volumes of virtual material. To use this feature, click Search & Explore in the Research & Learn channel and follow the instructions in the following Step-by-Step box.

STEP BY STEP **Conducting a Search**

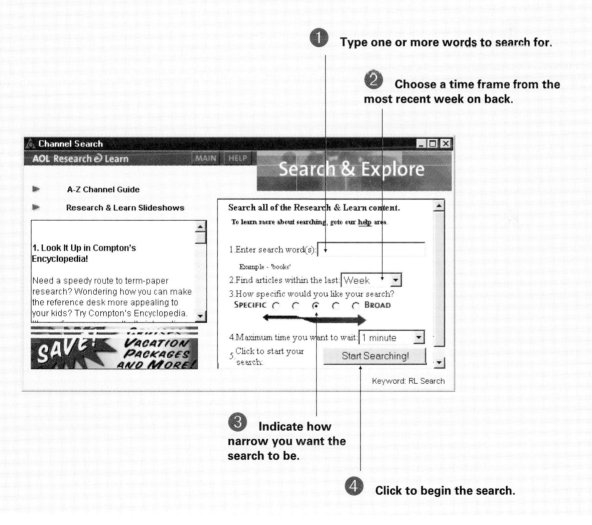

① Type one or more words to search for.

② Choose a time frame from the most recent week on back.

③ Indicate how narrow you want the search to be.

④ Click to begin the search.

EXPERT ADVICE

To make the most of your searches, take the time to familiarize yourself with AOL's search techniques. Click the underlined word Help *in the Search & Explore window to access Channel Search Help.*

A key advantage of online encyclopedias is that the publishers continually update them, so you'll always have timely information. In contrast, printed encyclopedias—and even those on CD-ROMs—go out-of-date pretty quickly.

Electronic Encyclopedias

The computer age has just about done away with printed encyclopedias—and no wonder. What's the point of buying two dozen heavy books when you can get the same information right on your PC. With AOL, in fact, you have a choice of three general-purpose encyclopedias—*Compton's Living Encyclopedia*, the *Columbia Concise Encyclopedia*, and the *Grolier Multimedia Encyclopedia*. The Compton's encyclopedia is the one best-integrated into AOL, and it's pretty cool, featuring 35,000 articles and 10 million words, along with photos, graphics, and maps. Want to know more about nuclear power? You'll find 170 entries, including the one shown in Figure 8.10.

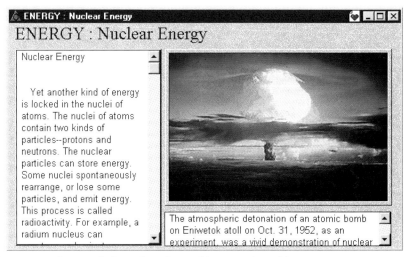

Figure 8.10 *Compton's Encyclopedia* combines words and images.

Who Needs a Copy Machine?

Here's another advantage the AOL Reference Desk has over a public library: When you want to copy something from an online encyclopedia or other reference work, you don't have to find a vacant copy machine and fish through your pockets for change. Just print the article by clicking the Print button on the toolbar while the article is displayed on the screen. You can also save it to your computer's hard disk by using the same technique described earlier for news articles.

SHORTCUT

Use the CTRL key in combination with other keys to manipulate text without taking your hands off the keyboard. For instance, press CTRL-C to copy text to the clipboard. Then open up a word processor and press CTRL-V to paste in the text.

Copying to a Word Processor

If you like, you can copy text from any AOL or Web-based reference work directly into a document you've created with a word processor. Just follow these steps:

1. Select the text you want to copy and then choose Copy in the Edit menu.
2. Launch your word processing program and open the document in which you want to insert the material.
3. Place the insertion point where you want the text to go and choose Paste from the word processor's Edit menu.

A Way with Words

As a writer, I always keep a dictionary handy. When I'm signed on to AOL, however, I don't ever reach for it because there's a great one online. It's the *Merriam-Webster Collegiate Dictionary* (see Figure 8.11), which you can access by clicking Dictionary in the Research & Learn channel. The dictionary contains more than 160,000 entries, and it's faster to use—and more useful—than a printed dictionary. Not only can you search for words, you also can find all entries in the dictionary that mention a particular word.

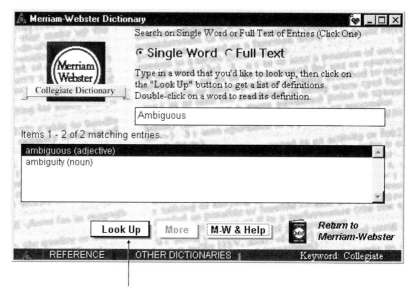

Click to display the definition.

Figure 8.11   Find the meaning fast with *Webster's* dictionary.

EXPERT ADVICE

Don't get rid of your printed dictionary! Unless you're already online, it's probably faster to look something up in a book than it is to sign on to AOL and find it in an online dictionary.

Other Online Dictionaries

AOL also offers other dictionaries, which you'll find by choosing More References in the Research & Learn channel (the list of dictionaries is shown in Figure 8.12). You'll find a dictionary for kids, a medical dictionary, and a bunch of Web-based dictionaries, including one devoted just to cheese—350 types, in fact. You'll also find the *Dictionary of Cultural Literacy,* a storehouse of definitions covering everything from mythology and folklore to popular expressions. Do you know, for instance, where the phrase "the real McCoy" comes from? According to the *Dictionary of Cultural Literacy,* it refers to a prizefighter named McCoy who had so many imitators that no one was sure who the real one was.

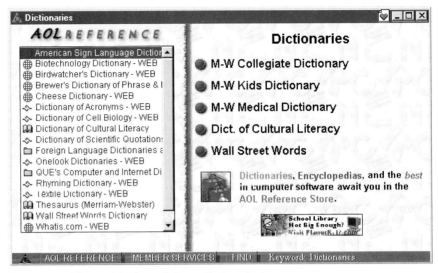

Figure 8.12 My word, look at all these dictionaries!

When the Right Word Eludes You Can't find just the right word to express yourself? No problem. Just click More References and you'll find the *Merriam-Webster's Online Thesaurus*—an electronic version of *Merriam-Webster's Collegiate Thesaurus*. It boasts more than 130,000 synonyms, antonyms, related and contrasted words, and idioms. It's similar to but better than the thesaurus in most word processing programs.

Reach Out and Touch Somebody

Need a phone number or an address? Take advantage of AOL's online directories, with which you can locate millions of people and businesses across the country (not that you'd want to). Click Phone & Addresses in the Research & Learn channel to display options that include white pages, yellow pages, a way to look up area codes, and even a zip code directory. Using the Switchboard Yellow Pages, you can even display a map showing the location of a business, as in Figure 8.13.

Other Basic Reference Works

Encyclopedias, dictionaries, and directories are just the start of AOL's online reference library. Let's take a look at some of the most interesting reference resources, IMHO (that's Internet lingo for "in my humble opinion").

You can zoom the map in or out.

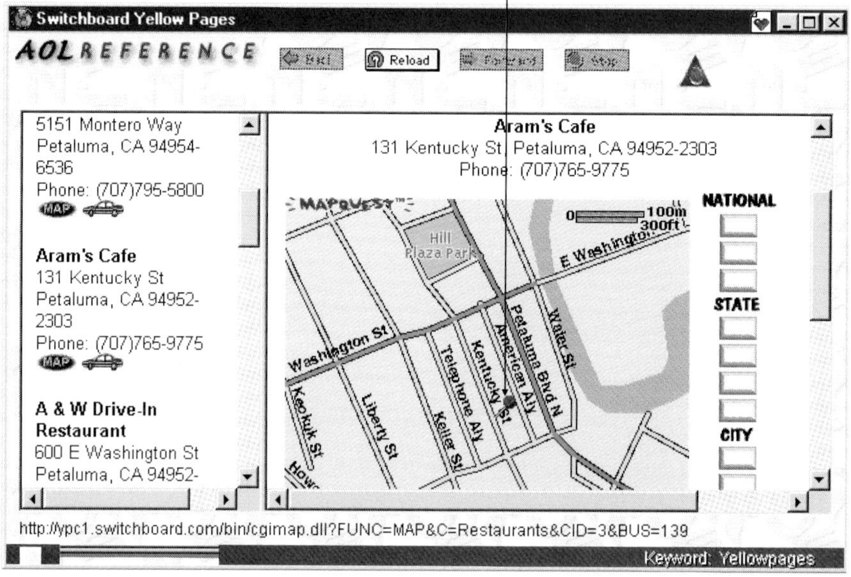

Figure 8.13 Here's how to get to Aram's, a nice little Armenian restaurant...

EXPERT ADVICE

By using an online white pages or yellow pages, you can save not only the time it takes to call directory assistance, but money as well, because most telephone companies now charge every time you call an operator.

The New York Public Library Desk Reference

Drawing from the resources of one of the world's great libraries, the New York Public Library Desk Reference, shown in Figure 8.14, is sort of a combination encyclopedia-almanac (just the thing to help you brush up for a big game of Trivial Pursuit or Jeopardy). It's organized into more than two dozen categories and features downloadable illustrations, tables, maps, and lists. And of course you can search for specific topics. The best part about this online library is that you don't have to go all the way to New York to use it. The NYPL Desk Reference can be found under More References in the Research & Learn channel.

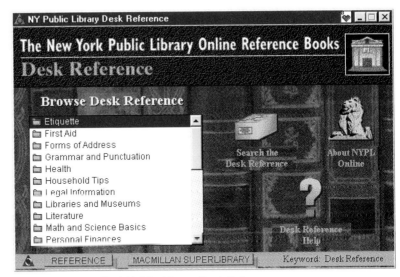

Figure 8.14 The New York Public Library Desk Reference

Who Needs a Lawyer?

At one time or another, almost everyone consults a lawyer. However, you may save yourself a fee and get answers to some legal questions by using the Nolo Press Self-Help Law Center. You'll find it under Legal Resources, which you can access by clicking More Subjects in the Research & Learn channel and then clicking Law & Government. This online law library offers information about everything from adoption to immigration. It can help you make out a will or take somebody to small claims court. There's even an area set aside for lawyer jokes, such as this one: What's the difference between God and a lawyer? God doesn't think he's a lawyer.

Sound Smart—Quote Someone Important

Nothing makes you look smarter than quoting someone smarter than yourself—and the best source for quotations is *Bartlett's Familiar Quotations* (see Figure 8.15). This is place to go for the wit and wisdom of Shakespeare, Churchill, and nearly every other famous historical or literary figure. You'll find *Bartlett's* tucked away in the Reading & Writing section of the Research & Learn channel. One question, however: Who was Bartlett?

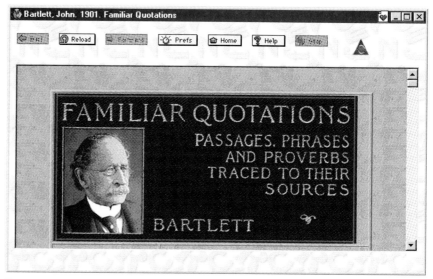

Figure 8.15 If it's a famous quote, it's probably in here.

EXPERT ADVICE

The Internet is a storehouse of reference materials, and it's easy to find them using AOL's NetFind (click the Internet button on the toolbar and then choose AOL NetFind). There are links to all sorts of encyclopedias and dictionaries, plus reference works on a variety of subjects. Also check out the big search engines such as Yahoo and Infoseek, which have lots of reference links.

Your Online Education Center

If you're like most busy parents, sometimes you don't have either the time or the energy to sit down with your child in the evening and pore over homework—especially when it comes to subjects like math, where you might not be much help even if you tried. Don't despair, however. Nobody's going to flunk as long as AOL is around. With the Ask-A-Teacher feature in the Research & Learn channel (shown in Figure 8.16), students—and parents—can obtain answers to

Ask-A-Teacher is free, which is amazing considering the cost of a private tutor these days.

homework and other academic questions in a number of ways. Just click Ask-A-Teacher in the channel window and pick the appropriate age group: Elementary School, Jr. High and High School, or College and Beyond. Each one lets you do the following:

- Send a question via e-mail and get a response from a volunteer teacher.
- Discuss your problem live in a tutoring chat room moderated by a teacher.
- Use academic message boards to get advice from other members.

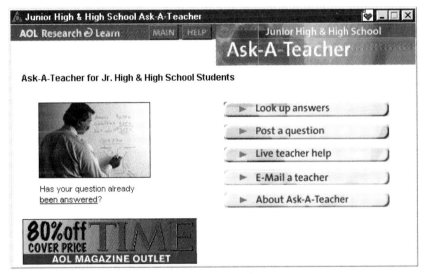

Figure 8.16 Kids can get help with their homework.

Check Out the Knowledge Database

In the areas for junior high and high school students and for college, you can also peruse an extensive knowledge database, which offers the answers to many often-asked questions. This is a good place to check before using other options, such as e-mailing a teacher. The database, shown in Figure 8.17, is fully searchable. To access it, click Look Up Answers in the Ask-A-Teacher window (for either junior high and high school students or college students) and then click the big question mark on the left.

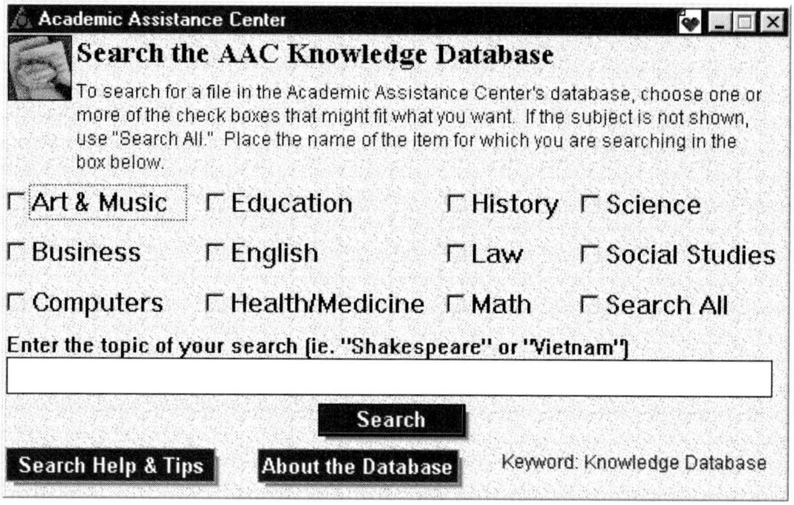

Figure 8.17 The Knowledge Database has all the answers.

Planning for the Future

What's the best college for you? How much does it cost to go? How and when should you apply? AOL can help you with these and other questions as you embark on the road to higher education. A good place to start is the area for the College Board, shown in Figure 8.18. The easiest way to get there is with the keyword **collegeboard**.

From here you can access the *College Handbook*, which contains descriptions of more than 3,200 colleges and universities. For each school you can learn about majors that are offered, admission requirements, athletics, and student activities. For instance, if you look up Harvard, you'll discover that in 1997 annual tuition and fees came to $21,901; estimated expenses, including books, supplies, and personal expenditures, excluding transportation, were $2,004; and room and board was $6,995. Whoa!

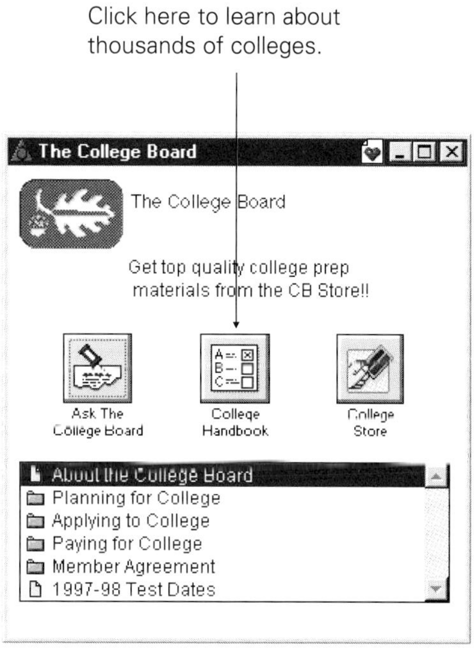

Click here to learn about
thousands of colleges.

Figure 8.18 The College Board area on AOL

EXPERT ADVICE

Need financial help with college? The Education section of the Research & Learn channel includes several good sources of information about scholarships, grants, fellowships, and other kinds of funding.

Enrich Yourself with an Online Course

AOL offers online courses on a variety of subjects such as English, math, art, computers, and business. These courses don't come with college credit, but they're a great way to continue your education in the comfort of your den. Classes include live, online lectures and message board and e-mail support. The registration fee for most courses is under $50, and classes usually meet online once a week for four or eight weeks.

CHECK POINT

After all this research, studying, and keeping up on the news, I think it's time for a break, don't you? Good, because in the following chapter, we're going to switch gears and have some fun. It's time for entertainment and sports, AOL-style. In fact, you could say it's just the ticket to a good time.

9

Your Ticket to Entertainment and Sports

INCLUDES

- Movie reviews
- Theater listings
- Popular music CDs
- Games
- Sports scores
- Following your team

FAST FORWARD

Check Out a Movie Review ➤ *pp. 194-196*

Want to see a review of a movie? Here's how:

New Movies

1. Go the Entertainment channel, click Movies, and then choose Critics Inc. from the More Flicks and Picks drop-down menu. You'll see a list of recent releases.
2. Double-click a title to see the review.
3. If the movie you want isn't listed, click Movies at the bottom of the window to access a more extensive list.
4. If you still can't find your flick, click Movies/Videos A-Z at the bottom of the New Movies window and search for the movie alphabetically.

Movies/Video A-Z   Critics' Ratecard

Find Out What's Playing at a Theater Near You ➤ *p. 196*

For nationwide movie theater schedules, do the following:

1. Click Movies in the Entertainment channel.
2. Open the More Flicks and Picks drop-down menu and choose Movie Listing - Movielink, which takes you to Movielink on the World Wide Web.
3. Click Search by Theatre, enter your zip code, and click Enter to see a listing of theaters in your area.
4. Click a theater to see the day's schedule.

Get the Lowdown on a New CD ➤ *p. 202*

No need to go to a music store to check out new pop recordings. With AOL, you can find out what the reviewers are saying and in many cases even download snippets of the latest albums. To check 'em out, click the Pop category in the Music section of the Entertainment channel and then double-click the New Releases folder in the list of resources.

Get Cheat Codes for Video Games ➤ pp. 204-205

Many video games have secret codes that let you give your characters added power and protection. The game makers don't tell you these cheat codes, but you can find them through AOL. One way is to visit the online version of *GamePro* magazine (keyword **gamepro**). Another is to check out game-oriented newsgroups on the Internet by double-clicking VGS Internet Connection in the resource list in the Video Games section of the Games channel.

Check the Scoreboard ➤ pp. 206 208

The first thing I do every time I sign onto AOL is check the sports scores. Here are three ways to do it:

- Click Scoreboard in the Sports channel (keyword **sports**) and choose the sport you want.
- Enter the keyword **scoreboard** from anywhere in AOL and choose the sport.
- Click the sport you want in the Sports channel, and then click Scoreboard. This is the same process as the first two steps, but in reverse.

scoreboards

- NFL
- NCAA FB
- MLB
- NHL

Join a Fantasy League ➤ pp. 208-209

Would you like to see how you could do as the manager of a professional baseball, football, basketball, or hockey team? Then AOL's Grandstand fantasy teams are for you. You can draft a team of top stars and then play against teams chosen by other AOL members in an online fantasy league. To join a league, use the keyword **fantasy** plus the sport you want, such as **fantasy baseball**.

Grandstand Fantasy Basketball
Get the inside info on your GFB draft in Pro/Fantasy Statistics

When you stop to think of it, entertainment and sports play an enormous role in the lives of most people, even busy ones, and there's no way you can keep up with everything—or can you? AOL lets you find information fast on everything from the latest blockbuster movies to the Super Bowl. There's news, features, gossip, and statistics in abundance, all easily accessible—and best of all: no TV commercials. That makes it ideal for busy people.

Entertainment

So you're a busy person. You still need to unwind once in a while by going to the movies, camping in front of a TV sitcom, or reading a good book. That's where AOL's Entertainment channel comes in (see Figure 9.1). It tells you all about the latest flicks, including where they're playing and whether they're worth going to see. You'll also find television listings for your area and best-seller lists to help you decide what to read.

Get the Inside Scoop

I don't know about you, but I love the movies—and AOL is the ultimate source for all things Hollywood. Just go to the Entertainment channel and click Movies. This will take you to the Movies window, where you'll find a wealth of information on your favorite films and actors. At the left side of the window you'll find a list of movies currently playing in theaters. Clicking a movie on the list gives you a rundown like the one in Figure 9.2 for "Boogie Nights." Notice that you can read reviews and a feature article, download a still shot, even download the trailer so you can view it on your PC.

Figure 9.1 The Entertainment channel

Stay on Top of the Hollywood Scene

The Movies window provides access to a wealth of Hollywood-related news and information. To view the possibilities, open the More Flicks and Picks drop-down menu. The list of resources includes *Entertainment Weekly, Hollywood Online, Premiere Online,* and *Newsweek.* There's also Critics Inc., a great place to

Figure 9.2 Find out the latest on all the latest films.

find reviews of hundreds of new and recent films as well as still shots that you can download. Here's how to use Critics Inc. to find a review:

1. Go to the Critics Inc. window. You'll see a selection of new releases. Double-click a title to see the review.
2. If the movie you want isn't listed, click Movies at the bottom of the window. That will take you to the New Movies window, which lists an extensive selection of recent releases.
3. If you're looking for a film that's been around for a while, click Movies/Videos A-Z at the bottom of the window and search for the movie alphabetically.

SHORTCUT

To quickly search for a movie review, click Search & Explore in the Entertainment channel and search for the title of the flick, making sure to choose the right time frame to search (All Articles is always a good bet).

Nationwide Theater Listings

How many times have you rummaged through the daily paper looking for the elusive movie theater listings? There's a much easier way, believe me. Here's what you do:

1. Click Movies in the Entertainment channel.
2. Open the More Flicks and Picks drop-down menu and choose Movie Listing - Movielink, which takes you to Movielink on the World Wide Web.
3. Click Search by Theatre, enter your zip code, and click Enter to see a listing of theaters in your area.
4. Click a theater to see the day's schedule, like the one shown in Figure 9.3.

Check Out the Coming Attractions

In addition to all kinds of stuff on movies that are already out, the Entertainment channel gives you the lowdown on flicks that are on the horizon. Click

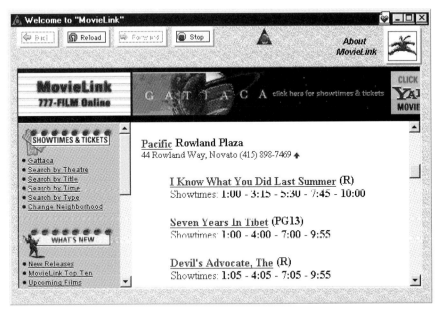

Figure 9.3 Local movie listings can help you decide what to see.

EXPERT ADVICE

Looking for information about a favorite actor or actress? The Web is loaded with pages about everybody from Marilyn Monroe to Brad Pitt. Don't forget that AOL NetFind can guide you to Hollywood-related sites.

Hollywood Online on the More Flicks and Picks drop-down menu in the Movies window and then click Coming Soon. You'll get sneak peaks at box office hits that are just around the corner, like the remake of "Flubber" starring Robin Williams (see Figure 9.4). You can also check out videos that are about to hit the rental stores.

Get the Most out of TV with Your PC

At first blush, it seems a little funny that you would use your computer to check out the world of television. But then again, why not? If you want the most up-to-date information of any kind, you're likely to find it online—and AOL delivers with TV Today, a section of the Entertainment channel. Here you'll find

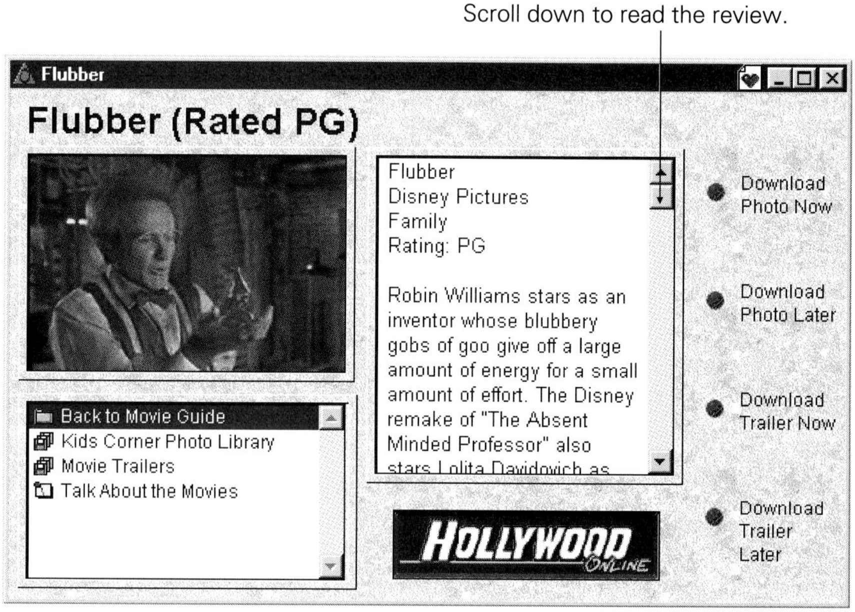

Scroll down to read the review.

Figure 9.4 Get the scoop on upcoming movies.

the latest news about some of your favorite shows, from soap operas such as "All My Children" to prime-time hits such as "ER" and "Friends" (see Figure 9.5). It's all there—information on episodes, the cast, the works!

TV Listings, Cyber-Style

Want to know what's on television tonight? Or when the big game will be broadcast? No problem. With TV Quest, you can view listings anywhere in the country. Just follow these steps:

1. Click TV Today in the Entertainment channel.
2. Choose TV Listings—TMS TV Quest from the More TV Features drop-down menu.
3. Click What's On TV.
4. Choose your city and click Continue.
5. Use the Channel Down, Channel Up, Earlier, and Later buttons to view different channels and time periods, as shown in Figure 9.6.

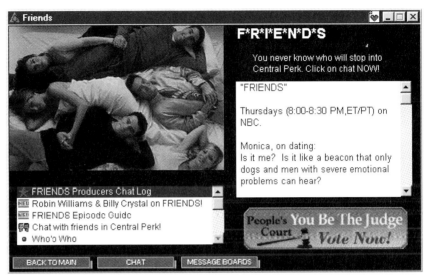

Figure 9.5 Keep up with "Friends" online.

Switch to another time period.

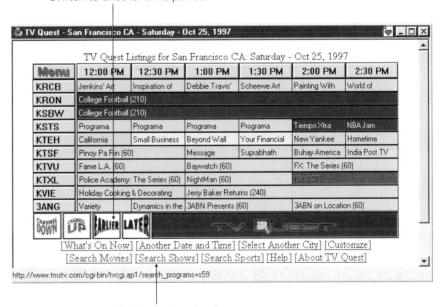

Find your favorite shows.

Figure 9.6 TV Quest is an interactive program guide.

"Star Trek" isn't the only TV show to have it's own fan club on AOL. "Frasier," "Mad About You," "Melrose Place," and "The X Files" all have online forums for fans. Enter the name of the show as a keyword to get there (for Melrose Place, just use melrose).

SHORTCUT

TV Quest lets you search for specific shows, movies, and sports events—simply click the appropriate search link at the bottom of the listings window. Just to see what would happen, I searched for "I Love Lucy" and found that, if I wanted to, I could watch 28 episodes in a single week.

Beam Me Up, Scotty!

One of the most popular of all destinations on AOL is the Star Trek Club, a forum devoted to the popular television series of the same name. Whether you're old enough to have been a fan of the original TV series or are a "Next Generation" lover, you'll find yourself right at home on this virtual USS Enterprise. You'll find the Star Trek Club, shown in Figure 9.7, by entering the keyword **trek**. Once there, you can beam yourself into a chat room full of Trekkers by clicking The Bridge.

Click to beam into the Star Trek chat room.

Figure 9.7 One of the most popular destinations on AOL

Don't Forget to Read a Book

The Entertainment channel may be heavily into movies and TV, but there's also room for people who still read books. If you want to see what's up in the world of literature, click Books in the Entertainment channel. That'll take you to the Books window, where you'll find reviews, best-seller lists, and links to literary magazines on the Internet.

Music to Your Ears

Music may be a universal language, but everyone has their own musical tastes. Fortunately, the music section of the Entertainment channel caters to all kinds of interests. It features areas for pop music, country (shown in Figure 9.8), classical, jazz, R&B, pop, and alternative rock. This is great for busy people, because it gives you ready access to information about your favorite kinds of music, both on AOL and the Internet.

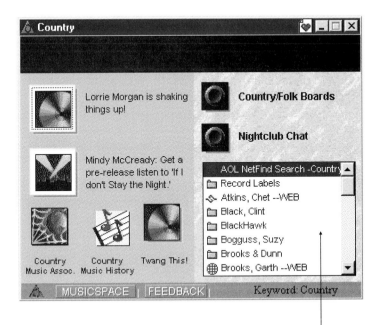

Find an artist on this list.

Figure 9.8 AOL's country connection

Scope Out the Latest CDs

No need to go to a music store to check out new pop recordings. With AOL, you can find out what the reviewers are saying and in many cases even download snippets of songs that will give you a good idea of whether a new CD is hot or not. Just click the Pop category in the Music section of the Entertainment channel and then double-click the New Releases folder from the list of resources. In Figure 9.9, we're taking a look at "Time Out of Mind" by Bob Dylan, who's been around for a long, long time.

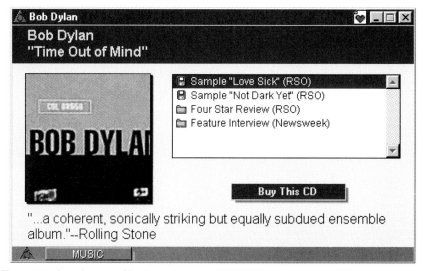

Figure 9.9 Popular new CDs have their own windows.

CAUTION

As you can see in Figure 9.9, it's possible to purchase music online (note the button labeled Buy This CD. This may be convenient, but keep in mind that when you consider shipping and handling costs, you'll probably pay more than if you shop around at your local music stores.

The "Long Strange Trip" Continues...

Not even the death of lead singer and guru Jerry Garcia seems to have fazed fans of the Grateful Dead. The band no longer performs, but its legion of camp followers still flock to the Grateful Dead forum to exchange memories and insights into the band that rocked the world for more than a quarter of a century. The forum, shown in Figure 9.10, contains chat rooms, message boards, and an online store where you can buy clothes, books, and other Dead memorabilia—oh, yeah, and albums, too. You can access the forum from the drop-down menu in the Music window or simply by using the keyword **dead**.

All the Coolest Games

Want to get your kids interested in computers? One sure-fire way is to turn them on to the Games channel, shown in Figure 9.11. Whether they like arcade-type action, role-playing adventures, or sports games, they'll find stuff here

Figure 9.10 Deadheads still flock to this AOL forum.

Figure 9.11 The Games channel has something for everyone.

to keep them in front of the computer for hours. In fact, it may ruin your busy schedule, because when you need the PC, junior will be using it.

Must-go places in the Games channel include:

- **Games Central**   The inside scoop on the latest hot games available for downloading on AOL
- **Video Games**   Loaded with previews, reviews, and the latest buzz about games for Nintendo 64, Sony Playstation, and Sega Saturn
- **PC Games**   News about new games for personal computers, as well as hundreds of games that you can download right onto your PC

Top Secrets You Can Have for Free

From watching my son play video games, I know that to get the most out them, you need to know certain secret codes that give your characters added power and protection. Game makers seldom tell you about these codes, even though they're built into the games. Here are a couple of good ways to find them:

- Check out *GamePro Online*, the AOL version of one of the best magazines on video games. This area, shown in Figure 9.12, offers candid reviews of all the latest games, features on the hottest

Hey kids! Click here for cheat codes.

Figure 9.12 The window for *GamePro Online*

technology, and lots of secret codes. You can access *GamePro Online* in the Video Games section of the Games channel or by using the keyword **gamepro**.

- Go to video-game-oriented Internet newsgroups, where experienced gamers share some of the best clues and codes. It's gotten so that codes for top games start showing up in newsgroups almost before the game is out. To access newsgroups for action games, double-click VGS Internet Connection in the resource list in the Video Games section.

Pay for Play: Premium Games

Most of the content on AOL is free, but if you want to play the latest, greatest multiplayer cybergames, such as Splatterball and Warcraft II, it's going to cost you

$1.99 an hour in addition to your regular monthly online fee. To enter the premium games area, find out what games are available, and play them, click Games Guide in the Game channel.

EXPERT ADVICE

Online gaming can be addictive, and that can add up to a nasty shock when you get your AOL bill at the end of the month. One answer is to block members of your family from playing games that carry surcharges. You can do this using the special section for Premium Services in Parental Controls.

The Latest on Sports

There are lots of ways to get sports news and information. The morning paper is loaded with stories about yesterday's events. Television stations provide regular updates. But if you want to know what's happening right now, the best place to go is AOL's Sports channel, shown in Figure 9.13, It's almost like being at the game, only you don't have to park or stand up for the National Anthem.

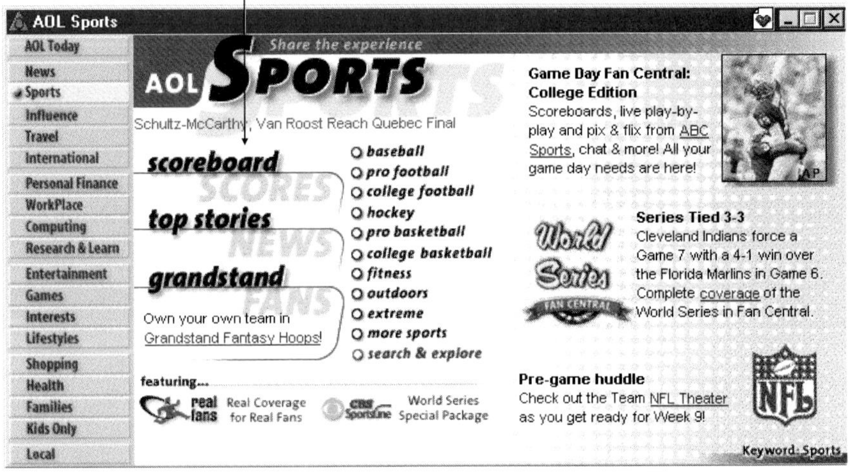

Click here for latest scores.

Figure 9.13 The main window for the Sports channel

News and Scores at Your Fingertips

For a quick look at the latest sports headlines, click Top Stories in the Sports channel. This is the place to go for hourly headlines and in-depth stories on the day's major events. Results of professional and major college events are put on AOL practically in real time. You can get scores in several ways:

- Click Scoreboard in the Sports channel and choose the sport you want.
- Enter the keyword **scoreboard** from anywhere in AOL and choose the sport.
- Click the sport you want in the Sports channel and then click Scoreboard. This is the same process as the first two steps, but in reverse.

Figure 9.14 shows you how scores are displayed. Note that in addition to final scores, you get scores in progress and schedule information for games that haven't yet started.

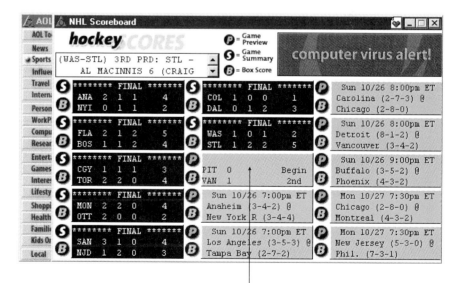

Current score for a game in progress

Figure 9.14 Get the latest scores all in one place!

SHORTCUT

If you're already perusing the News channel, you can cut right to the top sports stories by clicking Sports. That takes you to the same window that you get by clicking Top Stories in the Sports channel.

Follow Your Favorite Team

Clicking a sport in the Sports channel gives you access to league schedules, standings, and statistics—but that's not all. You can also go to an area devoted to your favorite team. There you'll find individual player statistics, box scores, injury reports, and historical analyses. Figure 9.15 shows the window for the world champion Chicago Bulls.

Join an Online Fantasy League

Ever wondered how you'd do if you were manager of a professional sports team? With AOL's Grandstand fantasy leagues, you can put yourself to the test.

Figure 9.15 Almost every team has its own area on AOL.

In a Grandstand league, you draft a team of top stars, which competes against teams chosen by other members. Grandstand leagues are available in baseball, football, basketball, and hockey. To sign up, go the fantasy area for the sport you want by using the keyword **fantasy** along with the name of the sport, for instance, **fantasy basketball**. There's only one catch: it costs $34.95 to register a team ($29.95 for baseball).

SHORTCUT

To access the AOL area for a particular big league team, try using the nickname of the team as a keyword. For instance, the keyword Bulls *takes you to the Chicago Bulls area, and* Yankees *takes you to the area for the New York Yankees.*

The Inside Scoop

AOL features areas dedicated to top athletes in many sports. To get there, choose Athlete Direct from the list of top sites in the sport you want. Figure 9.16

Figure 9.16 Everything you ever wanted to know about Troy Aikman

shows the area for Dallas Cowboys quarterback Troy Aikman. Many athletes keep online journals that provide a real insider's point of view. There are often cool photographs to download and message boards and chat rooms where you can discuss a player's performance with other members.

Special Sites for Special Events

Turn to AOL for up-to-the-minute news and online features about major sports events such as the Super Bowl, World Series, Wimbledon tennis tournament, Tour de France bicycle race, and Olympics. AOL creates special areas for these sports spectacles that offer some of the best coverage you'll find anywhere. Figure 9.17 shows the area for the 1997 World Series—a nail-biter if ever there was one!

Figure 9.17 The World Series, AOL-style

Not Just for Spectators

Sometimes it's a good idea to get away from your computer—but before you do, check out the Sports channel for the latest news and information about your favorite outdoor activity. From skiing to surfing, from mountain climbing to mountain biking, AOL has something for everyone. There's even a great area for snowboarding, the fastest growing of all winter sports. To access it, click Extreme in the Sports channel and then choose Snowboarding Online, shown in Figure 9.18, from the drop-down menu of top sites.

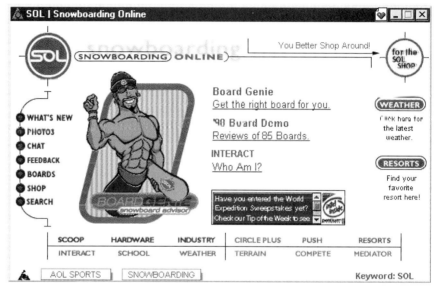

Figure 9.18 Have a nice time (but don't break a leg).

You Won't Find This in the Newspaper Most daily newspapers are pretty stuffy in that they don't think wrestling is a real sport. They argue that it's fixed. Of course it's fixed, but millions of people follow it anyway, and they want to know how Rowdy Roddy Piper and Jake "The Snake" Roberts are planning to dismember their next opponents. So here's what to do: click More Sports in the Sport channel and then choose Wrestling from the list of sports, or just use the keyword **wwf**. Either way, you'll go to the World Wrestling Federation area, shown in Figure 9.19. There you'll find message boards, a chat room, photos,

Click here for live online events.

Figure 9.19 Get ready, 'cause we're gonna rumble tonight!

sounds, video—even live online appearances by some of the biggest, baddest boys (and gals) in the business.

Meanwhile, Out on the Internet...

While AOL's sports menu is robust, there's an abundance of sports-related stuff on the Internet. AOL has links to some Web sites, but to get to many of the best sites, you have to know where they are. Here are the addresses for a few top sports sites:

ESPN	http://www.espn.com
CBS Sportsline	http://www.cbs.sportsline.com
USA Today	http://www.usatoday.com
CNNSI	http://www.cnn.com/SPORTS/
FOX	http://www.foxsports.com

CHECK POINT

Now that you've had your fill of sports and entertainment, it's time to get serious. In the next chapter, you'll see how to get expert financial advice, keep track of your investments—even do your own market research. Hurry—I think I heard the opening bell on the stock exchange!

10

Personal Finance Made Easy

FAST FORWARD

Create a Portfolio for Your Stocks ➤ pp. 220-222

It's easy to keep track of your stocks. Just create a virtual portfolio using the following steps:

1. Go to the Personal Finance channel and click Portfolios.
2. Choose Create Portfolio and give the portfolio a name.
3. Click Add Item.
4. Enter the name of the stock, the number of shares, and the price you paid.
5. Click OK. Repeat the process for each stock you want to add.

Check Out the Finances of a Public Company ➤ pp. 224-227

Suppose you're considering an investment in a company. Why not check out its financial condition first? Here's how:

1. Click Investment Research in the Personal Finance channel to open the Company Research window.
2. Click Financial Statements and then click U.S. Financials.
3. Enter the name or trading symbol for the company and click Search.
4. Double-click the name of the company from the list of search results.

Learn Which Mutual Funds Are the Best ➤ pp. 227-229

To view a list of the top-performing mutual funds, do the following:

1. Click Mutual Funds in the Personal Finance channel.
2. Click Morningstar and then choose Top-Performing Funds.
3. Double-click the category you want, such as growth funds.
4. Double-click the time frame, such as Ranked by 1 Year Return.

Put Your Bank Inside Your PC ➤ *pp. 229-230*

Online banking is becoming more and more popular, and AOL is at your service with home banking from more than two dozen financial institutions. You can check your balance, transfer money between accounts, and pay bills. Click Banking in the Personal Finance channel to see a list of participating financial institutions.

Get Help with Your Taxes ➤ *pp. 230-232*

The Personal Finance channel features a wide range of self-help tools for beleaguered taxpayers. You can download federal tax forms, get online advice, even download software to make tax preparation easier. Just click Tax Planning in the channel window.

Consult a Fool ➤ *pp. 233-234*

Need some good solid financial advice? Why not visit the Motley Fool, an area on AOL that offers savvy information about investing. You can learn about the market, find out why it behaves the way it does, and even share strategies and observations with other members. The keyword **fool** takes you straight to the Fool's lair.

If you're like most busy people, there aren't enough hours in the day to handle all the details of your personal finances. Wouldn't it be great if you could do your banking, investing, and planning for the future all in one place. Well you can by using AOL's Personal Finance channel. It can save you time as well as provide the tools you need to make wise decisions about your money—and with its vast collection of resources, it could even turn you into a financial wizard.

A Full-Service Financial Center

The Personal Finance channel, shown in Figure 10.1, is your gateway to just about every financial service under the sun. It lets you do your banking, track and trade stocks, handle your mutual funds, and research your investments, all without leaving your PC.

Market News at the Ready

If you've ever tried to follow the ups and downs of the stock market during the course of a day, you know how hard it can be. Even the best news-radio stations provide financial reports only a couple of times an hour, and in the evenings, after the markets close, it's almost impossible to find any business news—but with AOL, you can check up on top indexes any time you like. Current levels of the Dow, NASDAQ, and S&P indexes all appear in the main Personal Finance window. For a more in-depth look, click The Markets, which will take you to the Market News Center. Here, you can follow the world's major stock exchanges, such as the Japanese Nikkei shown in Figure 10.2. You can also get up-to-date information on currencies, futures, and bonds.

Up-to-date stock indexes
are displayed here.

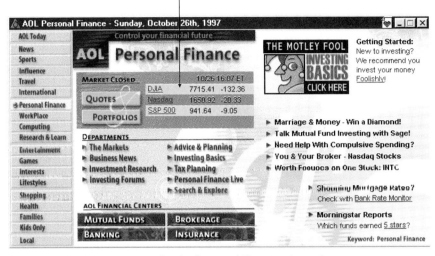

Figure 10.1 The main window for the Personal Finance channel

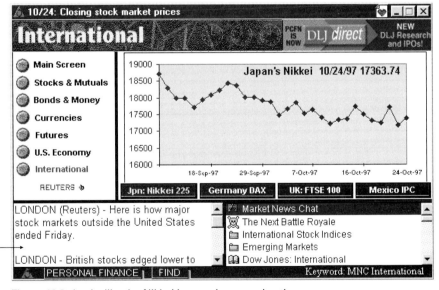

News summaries
from world markets
appear here.

Figure 10.2 Looks like the Nikkei is on a downward path.

DEFINITIONS

Dow: *The Dow Jones Industrial average, which includes some of the biggest stocks in the U.S.*

NASDAQ: *National Association of Securities Dealers Automated Quotation. A stock market that includes many smaller issues, but also a lot of big ones such as Intel and Microsoft.*

S&P: *Standard & Poor's. This index is often considered more reliable than the Dow in gauging the health of the market.*

Market quotes on AOL are delayed about 20 minutes. The same holds true for quotes that you can get on the Internet through such sites as Yahoo, Excite, and Infoseek.

Get a Stock Quote Fast

To get a quick quote on a stock, click Quotes on the AOL toolbar. That will display the Quotes & Portfolios window. Enter the ticker symbol for the stock, click Get Quote, and the most recent price will appear, along with information about the day's trading activity.

Tracking Your Stocks

If you own stocks or mutual funds, chances are you're constantly wondering how they're doing. More important, you're always trying to figure out how much money you've made or lost in the market. In the past, you had to wait for the morning paper to find out how your investments performed, and you needed a calculator to tally up your gains and losses. Not anymore. Just put your holdings in virtual portfolios and let AOL take care of everything. You can have up to 20 portfolios per screen name, with up to 100 items in each portfolio. To put stocks into a portfolio, click Portfolios in the Personal Finance channel and then follow the step-by-step instructions below.

EXPERT ADVICE

AOL lets you create multiple portfolios. You can use one for stocks you own, another for stocks you're following closely, and yet another for your mutual funds (even if they're part of an employee 401(k) retirement account).

STEP BY STEP Create a Stock Portfolio

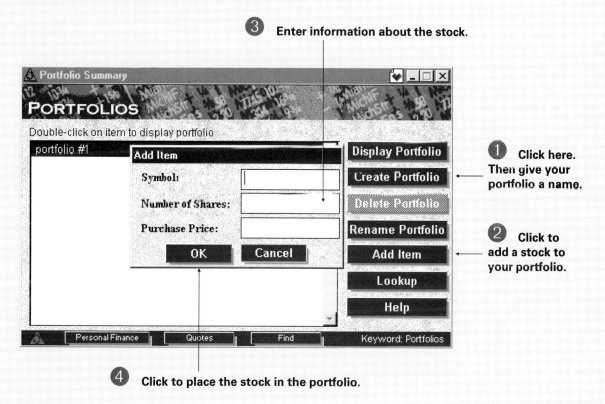

③ **Enter information about the stock.**

① **Click here. Then give your portfolio a name.**

② **Click to add a stock to your portfolio.**

④ **Click to place the stock in the portfolio.**

Viewing Your Portfolio

Any time you want to see how your stocks are doing, simply choose Portfolios in the Personal Finance channel, select the portfolio you want to view, and click Display Portfolio. You'll see a window like the one in Figure 10.3, which shows some stocks that I chose for a hypothetical portfolio (wouldn't you love to own these babies?).

Adding More Items It's easy to add an item to an existing portfolio. In the Portfolios window, just click the Add Item button and then enter the information for the new stock and click OK.

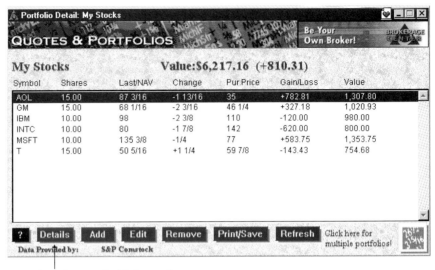

Click for detailed information
on a selected stock.

Figure 10.3 A blue-chip portfolio if ever there was one!

Trading Stocks Online

With AOL, you can actually buy and sell stocks online. In the Brokerage Center, shown in Figure 10.4, you'll find services from a number of first-rate brokerages, including Charles Schwab, E*Trade Securities, Inc., and Ameritrade. Trades can be placed anytime, day or night—which is a lot more convenient than hunting down a stockbroker—and the commissions for trades typically are less than if you use a real live broker. To get started, click Brokerage in the Personal Finance channel. Then choose an online broker and sign up for an account. Happy trading!

CAUTION

Trading stocks online is easy, but it can also be hazardous to your financial health. For all intents and purposes, you become your own broker when you do this, so make sure you're up to speed for the companies and industries in which you're trading.

Figure 10.4 Online stock trading is quick and inexpensive.

Market Research, AOL Style

There's no secret to solid investing, but it does take work. You need to thoroughly research every stock you buy—and AOL gives you the tools to do it. In fact, you have access to some of the same tools used by professional brokers and analysts. With them, you can perform all of the following:

- Track past performance of a stock.
- Check a company's financial history.
- View the latest financial results.
- Get analysts' earnings expectations.

EXPERT ADVICE

Daily financial news about the stock market and individual companies can greatly affect your investments. You can keep up-to-date with the headlines by clicking Business News in the main window of the Personal Finance channel.

Checking Up on a Company

To check out the financial health of a company, click Investment Research in the Personal Finance channel. This will display the Company Research window, shown in Figure 10.5. From this window you can conduct a wide range of research. Suppose, for instance, that you want to view a company's financial statements. Just follow these steps:

1. In the Company Research window, click Financial Statements. Then click U.S. Financials.
2. Enter the trading symbol or name of the company and click Search.
3. Double-click the name of the company from the list of search results (there may be other companies with similar names). This will provide you with annual income figures and balance sheets for the company, along with detailed information on liabilities and cash flow.

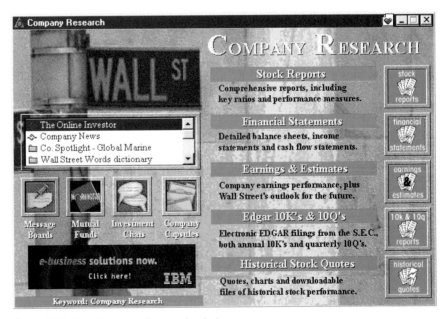

Figure 10.5 The Company Research window

Accessing the Government's Own Database

AOL offers direct access to EDGAR, the federal government's electronic filing system for documents that public companies must release. These include 10Ks (annual reports) and 10Qs (quarterly earnings reports). To access EDGAR, click the button for 10K and 10Q reports in the Company Research window. If you expect to find up-to-date information, though, forget it. EDGAR is typically several weeks behind, so the latest earnings report you're looking for may just not be there.

DEFINITION

EDGAR: *Electronic Data Gathering, Analysis, and Retrieval. This database is operated by the Securities and Exchange Commission, which oversees U.S. corporations.*

Company Profiles at a Glance

For general information about companies, the best place to go is Hoover's Company Capsules. These are smartly written summaries about corporations in many industries, complete with a list of key officers and numbers for getting in touch with the company. To access this feature, click the Company Capsules button in the Company Research window.

Great (and Not So Great) Expectations

Wall Street analysts make it their business to go out on a limb and predict per-share earnings for public companies. With AOL, you're privy to such forecasts, like the one shown in Figure 10.6. To see the latest expectations for a public company, do this:

1. Click Earnings & Estimates in the Company Research window.
2. Click Search Earnings & Estimates.
3. Type the company's name or ticker symbol and click Search.
4. Double-click the name of the company to display the estimates from First Call.

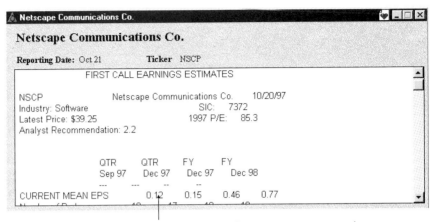

Earnings estimate for the latest quarter appears here.

Figure 10.6 Earnings estimates for Netscape Communications

SHORTCUT

Want all the latest news about a public company? The keyword company news *will take you to a window where you can use a company's stock symbol to view recent articles and press releases relating to the company.*

Viewing a Stock Chart

Past performance is no guarantee of future results, especially when it comes to Wall Street. However, it's often possible to spot trends based on stock charts. To create a chart of a publicly traded stock, do the following:

1. Click Historical Quotes in the Company Research window.

2. Enter the ticker symbol or name of the company you want to chart.

3. Select a time period for your chart (daily for a month, weekly for a year, monthly for three years—or specify your own parameters by clicking Custom).

4. Click Graph to create and display the chart. I created the graph shown in Figure 10.7 that shows the closing prices of Microsoft over three years.

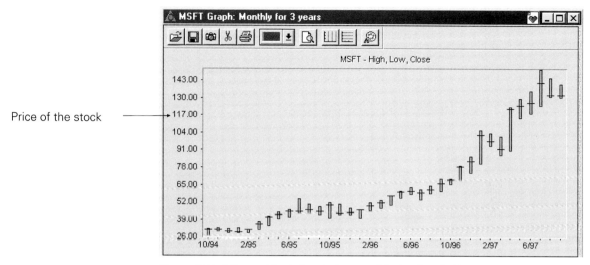

Price of the stock

Figure 10.7 Microsoft's obviously done well by its shareholders.

If you'd rather see raw data than a chart, click Quotes instead of Graph. The information will include not only closing prices, but also the volume plus the high and low for each date.

SHORTCUT

Historical stock data generated in AOL can be used in other programs. You can save stock charts as images, and tables of quotes can be saved and later imported into spreadsheet programs and financial software such as Quicken.

Mutual Funds

Americans are increasingly turning to mutual funds as a primary way to invest—and no wonder. Funds are less volatile and risky than stocks, so you can go to bed at night knowing you won't be wiped out in the morning. Many mutual fund companies now offer services on AOL. You can find out how individual funds are performing and even manage your own funds, buying and selling shares online.

Reflecting the growing clout of mutual funds in the marketplace, AOL has an entire area devoted to them. Click Mutual Funds in the Personal Finance channel to access the Mutual Fund Center, shown in Figure 10.8. You'll notice that several fund companies are showcased in the center, but you can view a complete list of available funds by clicking More Funds.

Click for a complete
list of online funds.

Figure 10.8   The place to go for mutual funds

Learning about Fund Investing

Don't know much about mutual funds? Don't worry. In the Mutual Fund Center you'll find a plethora of information and advice about investing in them. For example, T. Rowe Price provides areas called "Investment Fundamentals" and "Retirement Planning," and Dreyfus offers a comprehensive online guide to investing.

Rating the Funds

Want to know which funds are the top performers in their categories? You've come to the right online service, because AOL brings you Morningstar, an

DEFINITION

Mutual fund: A collection of stocks, bonds, or other securities managed by a professional investment firm. When you buy shares in a mutual fund, you're not pinning your hopes on a single security. Your gains and losses reflect the overall performance of the fund.

independent company that tracks and evaluates some 8,000 mutual funds. Morningstar is generally considered the top company in its field, and it has a sizable area on AOL. To access it, click the Morningstar button in the Mutual Fund Center window.

The Lowdown on High Achievers With Morningstar, you can search for individual funds to see how they're rated, or you can view a list of the top 25 performers in any category of funds (equity-income, European, growth, and so on). For example, Figure 10.9 shows the top overall funds during the past year as ranked by Morningstar. To view this list, do the following:

1. Click Top-Performing Funds in the Morningstar window.
2. Double-click Top 25 Overall Mutual Funds.
3. Double-click Ranked by 1 Year Return.

EXPERT ADVICE

To see how a mutual fund is doing on a daily basis, look it up the same way you would find a stock quote. Click the Quotes button on the toolbar, enter the ticker symbol for the fund, and click Get Quote. If you don't know the symbol, use Lookup or find it through Morningstar.

Home Banking

It used to be that every time you went to the bank, you wound up standing in a line. Then along came automatic teller machines and voila! Instead of standing in a line inside the bank, you got to stand in one outside. But banking doesn't have

	Morningstar Rating	Max Load	Total Return 3 Mo	Total Return 1 Yr	Annlzd Return 3 Yr
Lexington Troika Russia	--	12b-1	21.16	149.43	n/a
Fidelity Sel Energy Service	***	3.00	36.86	94.38	48.38
Hartford Cap Apprec A	--	5.50	22.12	90.54	n/a
Hartford Cap Apprec Y	--	None	22.23	90.35	n/a
Hartford Cap Apprec B	--	5.00	21.86	89.20	n/a
Fidelity Sel Brokerage&Invmt	****	3.00	23.29	81.53	37.11
Evergreen U.S. Real Estate Y	****	None	29.01	78.70	33.65
Evergreen U.S. Real Estate A	--	4.75	28.93	78.28	n/a
Evergreen U.S. Real Estate B	--	5.00	28.72	76.87	n/a
American Heritage	*	None	3.00	74.58	3.54
State St Research Aurora C	--	None	22.67	73.08	n/a
State St Research Aurora A	--	4.50	22.69	72.70	n/a
Parnassus	**	3.50	21.87	71.61	20.30

Figure 10.9 The top mutual funds over the past year

to be that way. More than two dozen financial institutions now offer online banking via AOL. It's a safe, easy way to handle your checkbook and other banking right from your PC.

Banking You Can Do Online

With an online account you can check your account activity (see Figure 10.10), transfer money between accounts, even pay bills electronically. And it's inexpensive—in fact, paying bills online can be less expensive than mailing checks. To investigate online banking, click Banking in the Personal Finance channel. If your bank is one of those listed, you can apply online for home banking (if not, you can start an account with any of the online banks).

Getting Help with Your Taxes

Preparing your income taxes can be the most perplexing, frustrating experience in the world. The tax regulations are so complicated they make you wonder

Figure 10.10 An online demo for Wells Fargo's home banking service

CAUTION

If you plan to pay bills through an online bank account, bear in mind that it takes most banks five to seven days to get a payment to a merchant. Also, some banks take money out of your account when the payment is sent, not when it clears the bank.

whether anybody can understand them—even the government that wrote them. If you've had it up to here with taxes, it's time to visit the Tax Planning area of the Personal Finance channel. This is the place to go for everything you need to make short work of your taxes, including:

- Federal tax forms and schedules (see Figure 10.11)
- The latest news affecting tax laws
- Plenty of online advice for taxpayers
- Software to help you prepare your taxes

Figure 10.11 Most popular federal tax forms are available through the Personal
Finance channel.

If you're really stumped, you can download the entire U.S. Tax Code by
double-clicking U.S. Tax Code On-Line from the list of resources in the Tax
Planning window

EXPERT ADVICE

*Official tax forms are formatted in Adobe Acrobat, a technology that lets
you make printouts that look exactly like the original. If you plan to
download tax forms, you'll also need to download and install the Acrobat
Reader software, which can be found along with the forms in the Tax Forum
or by entering the keyword adobe.*

Study Up on Financial Basics

If you're new to the investment game—or if you just want to broaden your
knowledge—click Investing Basics in the Personal Finance channel. In this

well-stocked area you'll find everything you need to become the next Warren Buffett. There's information on investment concepts and guidance on buying stocks, bonds, and mutual funds—and if you want to know what you're talking about, try brushing up on financial jargon with the Wall Street Words dictionary, shown in Figure 10.12.

Double-click to display the definition.

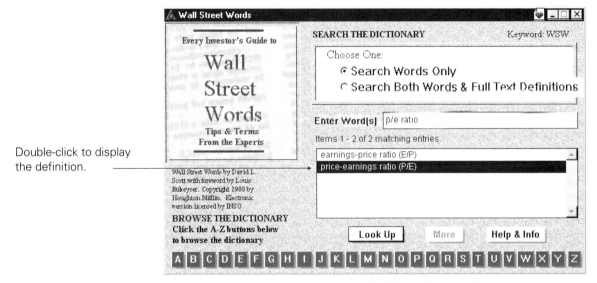

Figure 10.12 Master the jargon with the Wall Street Words dictionary.

These Guys Are No Fools

One of most interesting and entertaining areas anywhere on AOL is the Motley Fool forum. Started by two young brothers, Motley Fool is named for a line in Shakespeare's "As You Like It." Motley fools used humor to impart knowledge, and they could tell the king the truth without being punished. The philosophy of this latter-day fool is that individual investors can do just as well as seasoned professionals. Motley Fool's message boards, where you can share investment strategies and observations with other members, are among the most active on AOL. The easiest way to access Motley Fool's main window (shown in Figure 10.13) is with the keyword **fool**.

Figure 10.13 The Motley Fool is neither motley nor foolish.

Free Advice (Can't Beat That)

Wouldn't it be nice if there were somewhere you could go for free (and professional) advice on how to manage your money? A place you could get answers to questions about investing, taxes, and day-to-day finances? Well, there are such places, and you'll find them in Personal Finance Live, a collection of message boards and chat rooms in the Personal Finance channel. There, you can pitch questions and get answers about everything from stocks to small businesses.

There's more to life than making money, as you'll find out in the next chapter. We'll investigate Kids Only, Lifestyles, Health, Families, Interests, and Workplace—channels that cover just about every aspect of daily living, including romance, babies, jobs, hobbies, cars, and careers. That's a lot of stuff, so let's get going!

CHAPTER

11

How AOL Can Help with Real-Life Issues

INCLUDES

- Help for parents
- Kids' stuff
- Buying a car
- Online romance
- Health and fitness
- Businesses and jobs

FAST FORWARD

Research Your Family Name ➤ *pp. 239-241*

Ever wondered about the history of your family and your family name? The Genealogy Forum can help you dig into history and trace your roots. You can access lots of resources on the Internet, exchange information with other members in a chat room, and even check out research others have already done. To get to the forum, do this:

1. Click the Families channel in the Channels window.
2. Click Family Ties.
3. Scroll down the index and click Genealogy Forum.

Get Homework Help for Your Child ➤ *pp. 241-243*

Parenting is tough, and you don't always have the time to help your children with their homework. Don't worry, because AOL has the answer. With Homework Help, your elementary school child can conduct his or own research, get online tutoring, and even ask a teacher about a particularly knotty problem. You'll find Homework Help in the Kids Only channel.

Shop for a New Car ➤ *pp. 243-244*

Most people consider shopping for a car to be only slightly less distasteful than going to the dentist. AOL can't make getting your teeth fixed any more enjoyable, but it can sure take the pain out of buying a car. You can get all the facts about the car you want, including what the dealer paid for it, and you can even get a low price quote from a nearby dealer. Click Auto Center in the Interests channel and then click double-click AOL AutoVantage: New Car Buying.

Improve Your Cooking ➤ pp. 265-266

Busy people sometimes don't have much time for cooking, but that doesn't mean you shouldn't know how. With the Cooking Club, you can improve your technique in the kitchen by chatting with other members, going to Cook's School, and browsing through thousands of Online Cookbook recipes that AOL members have posted over the years. Click Food in the Interests channel and then scroll down and double-click Cooking Club in the list of food features.

Take Out a Personal Classified Ad ➤ pp. 268-269

Looking for Mr. or Ms. Right? Well, look no further. With AOL Classifieds, you can advertise yourself to the world and read personal ads posted by other members who live in your area. It's easy and inexpensive. You'll find the personal ads in the Romance section of the Lifestyles channel.

Find Out What's Ailing You ➤ pp. 269-271

Nothing's worse than being sick, but AOL's Health channel can help you find out about illnesses and their treatments. Here's how:

1. Click Illnesses & Treatments in the Health channel.
2. Double-click a category folder or enter a topic in the space above the list. Then click Search.

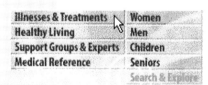

When you're not online, you're busy with your real life. AOL can't live your life for you, but it can help you deal with challenges, overcome obstacles, and in general make life easier. In this chapter, you'll take a quick tour of some of the channels that deal with real-life issues of family, lifestyles, health, and work. You'll discover that you can count on AOL for timely information and advice, and that you can also interact with other members who often are the best resources of all.

It's All in the Family

AOL has always been a family affair, and what better way to get the entire family involved than with the Families channel. Here you'll find information, support groups, and all sorts of goodies to help you make the most out of the time (all too rare these days) that parents and children spend together. One of the first stops you should make is Parent Soup, shown in Figure 11.1, an area that takes the guesswork out of raising kids. To get there, click Parent Soup in the Families channel window.

Moms Helping Moms

The best help in parenting often comes from other parents, and for that, the place to turn is Moms Online, which you can access most easily with the keyword **moms online**. This area includes several chat rooms where you can get together with other moms, as well as a feature called Ask the Pros, where you can use message boards to get advice from doctors, nurses, and other experts who happen to also be moms.

Figure 11.1 It's tough being a parent, but this makes it easier.

Name That Child

Parent Soup is especially good for new parents, who, as a general rule, have to learn by trial and error how to take care of new arrivals in the family. There's a club for new moms, where you can consult others in the same situation, and an area where you can learn about how to get through your pregnancy with a smile on your face. There's even a feature that helps you name your baby. Click American Baby in the Parent Soup window and then double-click Find a Name for Baby! You'll be able to find the origins and meanings of hundreds of names from Aaron to Zuriel. Figure 11.2 shows an example.

While You're At It, Find Out about Your Family Name

With the advent of the Internet, genealogy has become a growing interest because suddenly it's a whole lot easier to trace family histories—and AOL has an entire area devoted to genealogy, shown in Figure 11.3. To go there, do the following:

1. Click Family Ties in the Family channel.

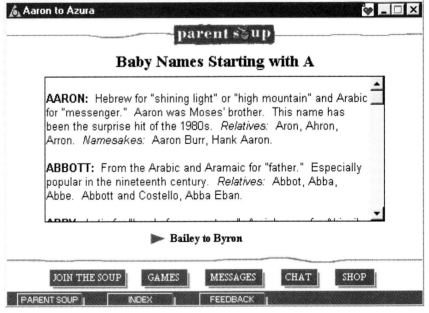

Figure 11.2 Learn the meaning of a name before you commit to it.

Figure 11.3 This forum will help you find out about your family name.

2. Click the arrow next to the button labeled "Index - Click Here for More."

3. Scroll down to Genealogy Forum and click it.

EXPERT ADVICE

The Genealogy Forum offers lots of resources both on AOL and the Internet. The first thing to do is to double-click Search by Topic in the forum's main menu. This will let you search for information that other AOL members have unearthed on hundreds of family names. Who knows—perhaps someone else has already done your research for you.

Kids Only

While we're on the subject of children, let's take a look at the Kids Only channel, shown in Figure 11.4. This full-featured AOL channel is strictly for the younger set, a place where they can learn and play online in a safe, secure environment. Here your child can get help with schooling as well as play interactive games that both teach and entertain. In Chapter 8 you learned how your kids can "ask a teacher" for help with homework. But that's just one of the many school-oriented features in the Homework Help area of the Kids Only channel. There's also quick access to a dictionary, encyclopedia, and thesaurus, and if your kids still need help, they can visit chat rooms where they can get online tutoring or share their questions with other members on message boards.

Play a Game and Learn at the Same Time

The Games area of the Kids Only channel lets children compete with each other online in games that demand quick thinking. There are contests that test knowledge of news, sports, and comics. One particularly cute game is Cranial Crunch, which is operated by Nickelodeon and draws hundreds of players at any given time. As you can see in Figure 11.5, it offers some pretty tough questions (the answer is Ghosts).

Figure 11.4 The Kids Only channel window

Join a Club Without Leaving the House

With 10 million members, AOL is a perfect vehicle for clubs devoted to a wide range of interests. In Kids Only, you'll find dozens of clubs for youngsters covering everything from computers to magic (some people think computers *are* magic). It's a wonderful way for kids to get together with other kids who have the

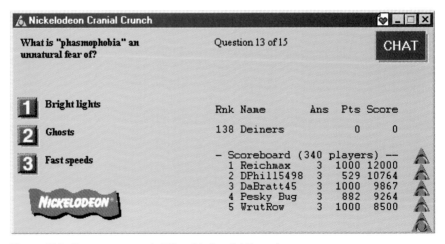

Figure 11.5 Test your mental skills with Cranial Crunch.

Figure 11.6 The AOL Computing Club window

If your children are 12 years old or under, you might want to restrict their online access to the Kids Only channel. To do this, you'll have to give each child a screen name and then go to Parental Controls, choose Set Parental Controls Now and check the box labeled Kids Only alongside the screen name.

same interests, and the real beauty of it is that club members can become friends even though they may be separated by thousands of miles. Figure 11.6 shows the Computing Club, where kids can exchange views with other members through message boards and chatting.

Food, Pets, Cars, Etc.

As a busy person, you probably spend a lot of your time at the computer doing work. But there's another side to life as well, and AOL has it covered with the Interests channel. This channel features areas on cars, food, pets, and hobbies—things that are important to almost everyone, no matter how busy they are. Let's look at a few ways in which this channel can help.

Buying a Car the Smart Way

People love new cars, but they hate the process of buying one. With AOL AutoVantage, you can take the guesswork out of shopping for a car and get a good price in the bargain. The AutoVantage New Car buying program is a free service that lets you find the car you want at a dealer near you at a low price. To get a dealer price quote on a new car, do the following:

1. Click Auto Center in the Interests channel.
2. Click Buying to go to the Buying Guide and then double-click AOL AutoVantage: New Car Buying to display the window shown in Figure 11.7.
3. Click Request a Quote. Then fill out the dealer referral form and click Send Request.

AutoVantage will respond to you by e-mail within a day, providing you with the name, address, and phone number of a local dealership, a contact person there, the AutoVantage preferred price, and any rebates that are available.

Figure 11.7 Use AutoVantage to make car buying easier—and less expensive.

How's the Fishing? Find Out Fast.

You're headed to Idaho for your annual fly-fishing expedition, but you aren't sure what to expect in the way of fishing conditions. No problemo. Fishing is just one of the pastimes covered extensively in the Hobbies section of the Interests

EXPERT ADVICE

Before you buy a car, click New Car Showroom in AutoVantage to find out about the model you're interested in. You can get the specifications on almost any car, plus valuable information such as a comparison between the dealer invoice price and sticker price that may help you drive an even harder bargain.

channel. Click Hobbies, scroll down the list of hobbies, and double-click the Fishing folder. Then click FBN, which takes you to the Fishing Broadcast Network, shown in Figure 11.8. There you'll find information on all kinds of fishing, including daily conditions for fly-fishing in every region of the country.

Figure 11.8 The Fishing Broadcast Network knows where they're biting.

Hungry? Visit the Cooking Club!

Even busy people have to eat, and there's nothing like a home-cooked meal. If you can cook, that is. To improve your culinary skills, visit the Cooking Club, shown in Figure 11.9, which you'll find in the Food area of the Interests channel. You can chat with other would-be five-star chefs and participate in the Cook's School, where expert instructions are available for things like roasting a turkey or decorating a cake. You can even peruse thousands of recipes submitted by AOL members over the years in the Online Cookbook, which happens to be one of the most popular message board areas on AOL.

Figure 11.9 Hone your culinary skills with the Cooking Club.

Lifestyles

One of the great advantages of being a member of AOL is the tremendous diversity of the online community. If you're interested in how other people live and what they believe, look no further than the Lifestyles channel. It covers a broad range of lifestyle issues, from traditional stuff like religion and romance to ethnicity and gay and lesbian lifestyles. Take Judaism, for example. Thousands of AOL members are Jewish, and many (like me) would love to know more about their religion and culture. With AOL it's easy. Just click Beliefs in the Lifestyles channel and then click Judaism. The available resources include Jewish Community, shown in Figure 11.10. Here you can find information on every aspect of Jewish life, including holidays, food, and Israel. There's even a matchmaking service, without which no Jewish community would be complete!

Figure 11.10 The place to come for all things Jewish

EXPERT ADVICE

Want to know a quick way to find stuff on topics that interest you? Use the keyword MYI, which displays a window called Match Your Interests. Here you can check boxes for categories like Health & Medicine and Hobbies & The Arts and get lists of cool AOL areas to explore.

The Love Connection

Speaking of matchmaking, AOL is a great way to start an online relationship (and in some cases, a real-life relationship) Who needs singles bars and blind dates when you can click Romance in the Lifestyles channel. Whether you just like to flirt or are serious about finding Mr. or Ms. Right, this area is just the ticket. In the Love@AOL area, you'll find message boards and chat rooms where you can share intimate thoughts with others on a variety of romantic topics. You can also take advantage of bountiful advice on how to be a great lover—not that you aren't already.

A Few Rules to Live (and Chat) By

Even though an online relationship is by definition a hands-off affair, AOL makes it clear that there can be danger involved. Here are a few tips on how to keep your romance a safe one:

- Remember that people you meet online are strangers, and in fact they may not even be who they say they are. A married man could be pretending to be single, and a man can even pose as a woman.
- Don't give anyone your telephone number or address online.
- Don't respond to a person who's lewd or crude. Ignore obscene e-mails and instant messages, or better yet, report such behavior to AOL by using the keyword **Notify AOL**.
- If you want to progress from an online relationship to a real-life one, be careful and use common sense. Meet in a public place and, if possible, in a group setting.

CAUTION

It doesn't happen often, but there are cases where young children have been seduced online into face-to-face meetings with child molesters. If you're at all concerned, use Parental Controls (keyword parental controls) to restrict you child's access to chat rooms.

When Online Isn't Good Enough

Okay, let's suppose you're not interested in an online relationship—you'd rather have the real kind. AOL can help there, too, with its online personal classified ads. AOL Classifieds are just like the classified ads in newspapers, except they're online. You can buy or sell a car or a home, find a job, or in this case, find a date or a mate. The service isn't free—at the time of this writing it costs $6.95 to run a personal ad for two weeks. But considering that millions of people may read your ad, it's a bargain. To access AOL's Romance Classifieds, shown in Figure 11.11, click Romance in the Lifestyles channel and then click AOL Classifieds: Romance.

Figure 11.11 Advertise yourself with a personal classified ad.

A Question of Health

Whether you're sick or well, health issues are probably never far from your mind. And whenever you have a question about your health, turn to the AOL Health channel. It's a comprehensive center for information, advice, and support on a wide variety of health and fitness issues affecting men, women, children, and seniors (that just about covers everybody).

Get the Scoop on an Illness

It's never enjoyable when you or someone you love is sick, but at least AOL takes the pain out of finding out about what's ailing you. To find explanations of common illnesses, as well as what to do about them, click Illnesses & Treatments

As plentiful as AOL's resources are, there's a whole lot more information about health and fitness out on the Internet. Links to useful Web sites can be found throughout the Health channel. You'll know a Web link because it's designated by a blue checkered circle.

in the Health channel. There you can choose from a list of categories covering everything from addictions to pain relief. Let's say your child suffers from asthma. To learn about this ailment, double-click the Allergies & Respiratory Disorders folder and then double-click the Asthma folder. This will display the window shown in Figure 11.12, which covers every aspect of that common childhood condition.

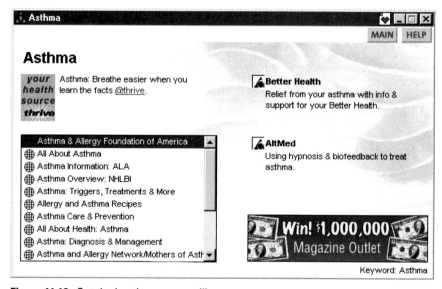

Figure 11.12 Get the lowdown on any illness.

SHORTCUT

If you don't want to click through the categories in the Illnesses & Treatments window, type the medical term you're looking for and click Search. That will take you straight to the resources for that condition.

Support Is Just a Click Away

Not only can you learn all about an illness and how to care for someone who has it, you can also get support from others who have dealt with the same problem. Click Support Groups & Experts in the Health channel to gain access to chat rooms where you can exchange questions and answers with other members. You can also send questions electronically to medical experts in a variety of fields. Some respond personally to you, while others post answers to selected questions.

The Keys to Staying Healthy

The best way to deal with sickness is to avoid it, and AOL can help there as well. Clicking Healthy Living in the Health channel will lead you to information on a number of topics, including eating well, fitness, and alternative medicine. Another good place to go is Thrive@AOL, which you can reach most easily with the keyword **thrive**. This area, shown in Figure 11.13, is a comprehensive resource for a healthy life.

Figure 11.13 It's easier to thrive if you're healthy and fit.

Work, Work, Work...

When you're not at home with the kids, you're probably at work. And whether you work in a big office, on a construction site, or in your own den running a home business, AOL's Workplace channel offers resources to make your professional life a whole lot easier. You can do research on public companies using many of the same tools found in the Personal Finance channel. In addition, the Workplace channel contains a department called Professional Forums, shown in Figure 11.14, which contains virtual communities covering more than 100 occupations, from accounting to veterinary medicine.

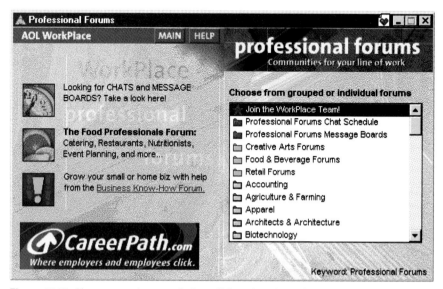

Figure 11.14 No matter what you do for a living, there's probably a forum for you.

Professional Forums provide links to sites around AOL and out on the Web related to your profession, as well as message boards that let you share ideas and get advice from other AOL members. And if you want to discuss issues in real-time, check out the Professional Forums chat schedule. Each week, two hours of chat are set aside for each occupation.

Running Your Own Business

Managing your own business can be a stressful and lonely experience—but never fret, because help is just a couple of mouse clicks away. Simply click Your Business in the Workplace channel to display the window shown in Figure 11.15. You'll find a cornucopia of information that can prove valuable whether you're starting a new business or trying to get the most out of an existing one. There's even a section on how to do business online.

Figure 11.15 If you have your own business, or you plan to start one, check this out.

A Good Career Move

Thinking about changing jobs? Click Your Career in the Workplace channel to display a window (similar to the one in Figure 11.15) that's focused on personal careers. Whether you want to advance in your present occupation or change directions entirely, you'll find the information to get the job done. There's even a section called Regional Resources that's loaded with Web links to state, county, and city employment agencies and other job-related organizations across the country.

Family and work can sure tire a body out. And when you're pooped, nothing fills the bill like travel and shopping. Which, it just so happens, are the topics of the next, and final, chapter of this book. Let's go!

CHAPTER

12

Travel and Shopping—The Really Fun Stuff

INCLUDES

- Making airline reservations
- Planning a getaway
- Touring digital cities
- Exploring foreign lands
- Shopping

FAX

FAST FORWARD

Important System <u>Update</u>

Reserve Your Flight ➤ *pp. 258-260*

Use AOL's Preview Travel feature to reserve and purchase your own airline tickets. It's easy! Just follow these steps:

1. Click Preview Travel in the Travel channel and then click the button for airline tickets, hotel reservations, or car rentals.
2. Create a travel profile for yourself and anyone else traveling with you.
3. Proceed to find flights that go where you want to go, when you want to go.

Find a Bargain Fare Fast ➤ *p. 261*

today's lowest airfares from preview travel

Listed below are sample fares available from selected airports. All flights are round-trip. This list updated 11/2/97 2:04PM.

* San Diego - Los Angeles for 87.00
* Boston - Dallas for 204.50
* Atlanta - Washington, DC for 144.00
* Orlando - Chicago for 272.00
* Philadelphia - Phoenix for 190.00

Use Preview Travel's Farefinder to quickly pin down the lowest available flights to major U.S. cities and favorite holiday destinations. Or go to Microsoft Expedia on the Web at www.expedia.com to search for low-priced flights anywhere in the world.

Check Out the Local Action with Digital City ➤ *pp. 264-265*

digitalcity
SAN FRANCISCO

Come join all the fun chats!

Today
- Cheers! Here's to savoring a FREE Wine Country Vacation.
- Get out of Dilbert-ville. Find a more fun, better paying job here.

Categories
- ☑ News & Sports
- ☑ Entertainment
- ☑ Real Estate
- ☑ Chat
- ☑ People
- ☑ Auto
- ☑ Travel
- ☑ Hangout
- ☑ Careers

Find out what's happening in more than a dozen major cities around the country with Digital City. Just click the Local channel and choose the city you want. You'll find a virtual community filled with the latest local news, sports, and entertainment, as well as the lowdown on the area's cultural and social scenes.

Check Out Paris ➤ pp. 265-268

The International channel is loaded with information about popular destinations such as London, Paris, Rome, and Tokyo. Just click the Travel department in the channel and then double-click the Tourist Attractions folder. You'll find some great resources that can help you plan where to stay, where to eat, and what to see.

Take AOL Along for the Journey ➤ p. 268

If you have a laptop computer, you can use AOL in most major cities worldwide. That means you can stay on top of the news, surf the Web, and exchange e-mail with people thousands of miles away. All you have to do is connect through the local AOL access number wherever you are. Just get the access numbers (use the keyword **international access**) before you travel.

Getting Started
Steps to connect to AOL from around the world.

Search for a Number
Need an access number for an International location? They are here.

International Access FAQ
All you need to know about using International Access is here.

Go on a Shopping Spree ➤ pp. 268-272

Feel like shopping? Then head to AOL's Shopping channel for some new clothes, perhaps, or maybe some nice chocolates. Here's how to make a purchase online:

1. Browse through the various departments in the channel or find a particular online store by using Search & Explore.
2. Once you've found an item you'd like to buy, you can order it immediately. Just click the order button and follow the instructions for completing the order.
3. You can also order other items from multiple stores. Everything goes into a virtual shopping cart. When you're finished, click Checkout and complete the purchases with your credit card.

Browse and shop around the clock!

AOL Shopping

What's in store today

➤ *Hot Savings* Deal of the Day - BIG Savings.
➤ *Shopping Services* Need your closest mall?
➤ *Classifieds* Need a new Job? Place an ad.
➤ *Shop Talk* Chat LIVE with us tonight at 9 PM EST.

What do busy people do when they aren't busy working? They're busy having fun, that's what. And since you've worked so hard while reading this book, it's time to do just that. In this final chapter, you'll learn how the Travel, Local, and International channels can help you plan your next vacation (or even make a business trip more enjoyable). Then you'll finish up with the Shopping channel, an extensive and secure online shopping area in which you can buy anything from a teddy bear to a computer modem.

Off We Go!

Whether you're packing for a trip or just wishing you were someplace else, AOL's Travel channel, shown in Figure 12.1, is just the ticket. Through this virtual gateway you can learn about great vacation spots, put together a dream trip, and even take care of plane tickets, hotels, and rental cars.

Who Needs a Travel Agent?

To plan a vacation or business trip, you ordinarily would have to call a travel agent and go through a laundry list of questions about when and where you want to travel. Then you have to wait while the agent tries to find the lowest-priced flights for you. But guess what—the agent is using a computer to look through a database of available flights and other information. You can do the same thing yourself, using AOL. Click Reservations Center in the Travel channel for a full rundown of the possibilities. Or click Preview Travel in the Travel channel to go to one of the most comprehensive, easy-to-use online travel services in existence. Preview Travel lets you easily shop for airline tickets as well as hotel and car reservations.

Figure 12.1 The main window for the Travel channel

AOL members can also reserve flights through American Express's ExpressNet service, which you'll encounter in the Reservations Center area of the Travel channel. But there's a catch: to use this feature, you have to have an American Express card.

Setting Up a Travel Profile

In the Preview Travel window, click the area for airline tickets, hotels, and rental cars. Before setting up your itinerary, you'll be asked for some information, including:

- Your mailing address, age, and daytime and evening phone numbers
- The class of service you prefer: coach, business class, or first class
- Your seat preference: aisle, window, and so forth
- Any special meal requests: kosher or low-cholesterol, for instance
- Your frequent-flier account information, if applicable

Booking Your Tickets

After completing this personal travel profile, you'll be led through a series of questions to find flights and book your reservations. You can also purchase the tickets online, using your credit card. Preview Travel will send the tickets to you by mail, or by express air if time is short. To reserve a flight, indicate where and when you want to travel. A list of available flights will appear in the window. Then follow the step-by-step instructions.

STEP BY STEP Reserving Airline Tickets

① **Select the flight you want and then click here.**

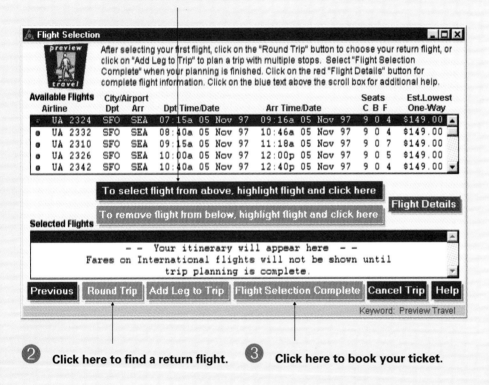

After selecting your first flight, click on the "Round Trip" button to choose your return flight, or click on "Add Leg to Trip" to plan a trip with multiple stops. Select "Flight Selection Complete" when your planning is finished. Click on the red "Flight Details" button for complete flight information. Click on the blue text above the scroll box for additional help.

Available Flights Airline	City/Airport Dpt	Arr	Dpt Time/Date	Arr Time/Date	Seats C B F	Est.Lowest One-Way
UA 2324	SFO	SEA	07:15a 05 Nov 97	09:16a 05 Nov 97	9 0 4	$149.00
UA 2332	SFO	SEA	08:40a 05 Nov 97	10:46a 05 Nov 97	9 0 4	$149.00
UA 2310	SFO	SEA	09:15a 05 Nov 97	11:18a 05 Nov 97	9 0 7	$149.00
UA 2326	SFO	SEA	10:00a 05 Nov 97	12:00p 05 Nov 97	9 0 5	$149.00
UA 2342	SFO	SEA	10:40a 05 Nov 97	12:40p 05 Nov 97	9 0 4	$149.00

To select flight from above, highlight flight and click here

To remove flight from below, highlight flight and click here

Flight Details

Selected Flights

```
- - Your itinerary will appear here  - -
Fares on International flights will not be shown until
trip planning is complete.
```

| Previous | Round Trip | Add Leg to Trip | Flight Selection Complete | Cancel Trip | Help |

Keyword: Preview Travel

② **Click here to find a return flight.**   ③ **Click here to book your ticket.**

CAUTION

Restricted fares are usually much less expensive than unrestricted fares, but you can fly only at certain times, and in many cases the tickets are nonrefundable. Be sure to familiarize yourself with any restrictions before booking a low-cost flight.

Finding the Lowest Fares Fast

There's nothing quite as satisfying as a really low air fare—it makes the whole trip worthwhile. With Preview Travel's Farefinder feature, you can locate the best possible fares to selected major cities and vacation spots in just seconds. Also check out the Bargain Box, which you'll find by clicking Travel Bargains in the Travel channel. It pinpoints special deals you can get on air travel and vacation packages.

Other Online Travel Services While Preview Travel is efficient and reliable, it isn't the only way to go. Several other travel services have sprung up on the Internet, and in some cases, they offer features you can't get on Preview. One of the best is Microsoft's Expedia (www.expedia.com). It provides a very fast way to find the lowest-priced flights anywhere in the world, and it displays the information quite nicely. Figure 12.2, for instance, shows the cheapest round-trip flights between San Francisco and London.

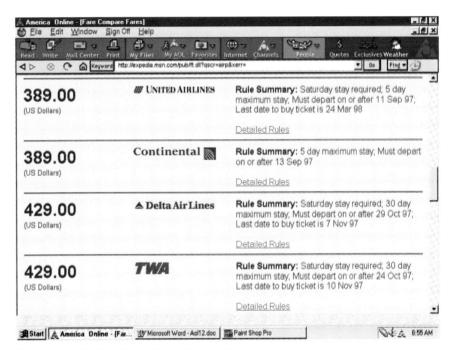

Figure 12.2 Find low fares fast with Expedia.

Don't Forget the Hotel and Car

After you've made your airline travel plans with Preview Travel, you can add a rental-car reservation, choosing from all the major rental companies—Hertz, Avis, National, Budget, Alamo, and so on. You'll get guaranteed rates and confirmed reservations worldwide. You also can find a hotel anywhere in the world, choosing from hotel chains such as Hilton, ITT Sheraton, Best Western, and Hyatt. You can check prices and availability of rooms, and in many cases, you can make the reservations online.

Planning a Getaway

Suppose you're going on vacation and want to check out your destination in advance. Well, you can forget brochures and guidebooks, because AOL has some of the best travel resources available anywhere. Just click Where to Go What to Do in the Travel channel and then pick your place. If you double-click the folder for the United States, you'll see a listing that includes Travel America, which offers all kinds of information on U.S. destinations. Figure 12.3 shows the Travel America area on Arizona.

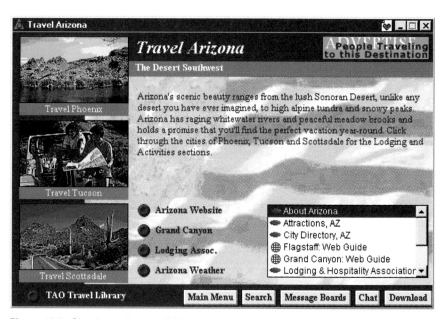

Figure 12.3 Check out the possibilities in Arizona with Travel America.

EXPERT ADVICE

AOL has members who have been just about everywhere. So check out Messages & Chat in the Travel channel. You'll find message boards and online discussions about every possible destination, from Alaska to Zanzibar.

Finding a Good Bed and Breakfast

Over the past few years, an increasing number of travelers have sought out the intimate atmosphere of bed-and-breakfast inns rather than cooping themselves up in big hotels—and in some remote areas, B&B's are the only places to stay. The problem has been how to find them, but AOL has the answer: Pamela Lanier's Bed & Breakfast Guide to over 14,000 inns around the world—including five in Skagway, Alaska. Check out this nifty site—shown in Figure 12.4—by using the keyword **B&B**.

Figure 12.4 An online guide to 14,000 B&Bs worldwide

Digital City—Also Known as the Local Channel

A great source of information about major cities is the Local channel. This is really just the old Digital City channel from the previous version of AOL. By calling it Local, AOL is emphasizing that it's the place for folks to turn to for news and information about their metropolitan area. As you saw in Chapter 8, the Local channel provides the latest local news. But it's also perfect for travelers who want to scope out a city before going there. There are Digital City areas for New York, Los Angeles, San Francisco, Philadelphia, Washington, D.C., and lots of other cities. Figure 12.5 shows Digital City Boston.

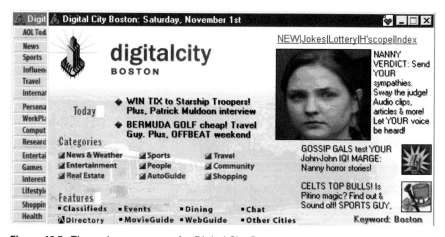

Figure 12.5 The welcome screen for Digital City Boston

It's Just Like Being There

The typical Digital City features key information including:

- News, weather, and sports
- A calendar of events
- A rundown of top restaurants and night spots
- Classified ads

- Chat rooms where you can trade banter about the local scene

In some digital cities you can even find out how bad the traffic is, as shown in Figure 12.6. Then you'll remember why you left the city in the first place.

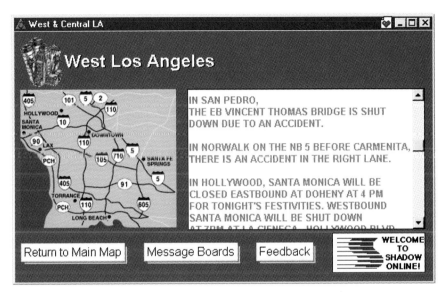

Figure 12.6 Looks like a typical day in the Los Angeles area.

Digital cities also have sprung up overseas. There are currently three for the British Isles—London, Glasgow, and Edinburgh— plus ones for Marseilles and Lyon, in France.

Local Stuff on the Internet

Digital City isn't your only choice for local information about big cities. Several competing services have sprung up on the World Wide Web. The best of them include:

- **Sidewalk.com** (www.sidewalk.com) from Microsoft
- **Citysearch** (www.citysearch.com)
- **Yahoo** (www.yahoo.com), which offers local sites for many cities

The International Connection

Okay, so much for the United States. If you're headed overseas, check out the International channel, shown in Figure 12.7. You'll find news and information about nations you didn't even know existed—there are even special versions of

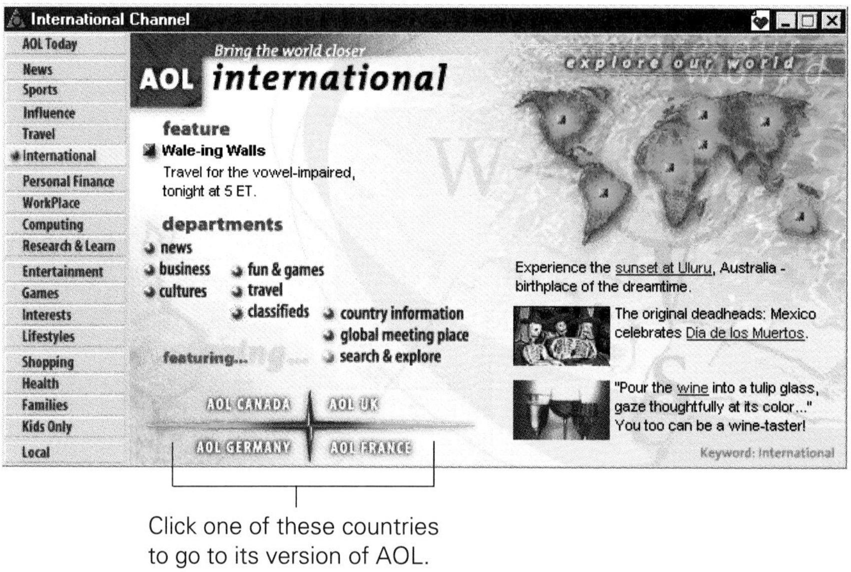

Figure 12.7 The main window for the International channel

AOL for Canada, the United Kingdom, France, and Germany. Or choose a geographical area on the map to home in on a particular country. Most countries have their own windows where you'll find useful information about travel, plus a map of the country. In many cases, you can even download the country's national anthem—though why anyone would want to do that is beyond me.

SHORTCUT

To go directly to information about a specific country that doesn't have its own area on AOL, try using the country's name as a keyword. In most cases, that will take you to a window devoted to information about the country.

London, Paris, Rome, Etc.

One of the easiest ways to get ready for an overseas vacation is to do the following:

1. Click the Travel department in the International channel.

2. Double-click the item titled Tourist Attractions.

From the list that's displayed, you can access the lowdown on lots of fabulous places. Want to check out Paris? Two wonderful online guides are right there: Bonjour Paris and Paris by AOL France (shown in Figure 12.8). Double-click either one for up-to-date information on hotels, dining, museums, and landmarks.

Figure 12.8 Discover Paris before you even get there!

Fast Facts about Faraway Places

One of the best resources for foreign travel on AOL is Lonely Planet, which you'll find in several places in the International channel or by using the keyword **lp**. Lonely Planet offers concise travel information on dozens of countries, including the history of the place, what it costs to visit, and when's the best time to go. And the best part is that all this information and advice is free.

What's Your Money Really Worth? Before traveling to distant lands, it's always a good idea to find out how far your U.S. dollars will go. Fortunately, AOL gives you a quick way to see how the dollar stacks up against foreign currencies. Just do the following:

1. Click Business in the International channel.
2. Double-click the Currency & Money folder.
3. Double-click Currency Conversions.

This will take you to a Web site where you can easily determine how many British pounds, German marks, Japanese Yen, or other kinds of currency there are to the dollar—and vice versa.

You can also access the currency converter through the Travel channel. Click Where to Go What to Do, click Know Before You Go, and then double-click Currency Converter.

Take AOL Along with You

One of the biggest benefits of AOL's global presence is that you can use it almost anywhere in the world. It's great for business people who want to stay in touch, and even for vacationers. When my wife and I went to Europe, we took a laptop computer and were able to exchange e-mail with our teenage sons. We'd tell them about all the places we'd seen, and they'd message back one-word replies like "Cool!" We simply logged onto AOL through local numbers in Germany, Switzerland, and France. To find international access numbers, use the keyword **international access**.

EXPERT ADVICE

Whether you're traveling abroad or just out of state, make sure to print out local AOL access numbers for the places you'll be visiting before you go. You can get them by using the keyword access.

Online Shopping

If there's one thing people like as much as traveling, it's shopping—which brings us to the Shopping channel (shown in Figure 12.9), our final destination. (I saved this for last because if we'd checked it out first, you would have already spent all your money and lost interest in the rest of the book.) Seriously, though, AOL offers a huge virtual shopping mall that's open 24 hours a day, every day.

Click for a list of online stores.

Figure 12.9 If you've ever wondered what a virtual mall looks like, this is it.

Where to Find Stuff? Everywhere!

You've probably noticed that no matter where you go in AOL, somebody's trying to sell you something. For instance, you can buy games in the Games channel and computer hardware and software in the Computing channel. You can even buy music in the Entertainment channel. But for the true shopping experience, nothing beats the Shopping channel, where you'll find merchandise from some of America's most popular merchants. Here's just a partial list:

- Eddie Bauer
- Land's End
- JC Penney
- L.L. Bean
- The Sharper Image
- Warner Bros.
- 1-800-Flowers
- Godiva
- Starbucks
- Tower Records

Online store fronts, such as the one in Figure 12.10, are among the most enticing areas on AOL—which figures, since the companies are trying to entice you into buying their products.

Figure 12.10 Who could resist a store as colorful as this one?

Browsing through the Virtual Mall

The Shopping channel is divided into areas such as Apparel & Accessories, Gifts, Books, and Music & Video. Each area contains links to merchants whose products fit the category. Go ahead and look around till you find something you want. Okay, that's enough—I haven't got all day. I'll tell you what—why don't I pick something so you can see how the online shopping process works? I'll choose something just about everybody likes—coffee. In fact, as you can see in Figure 12.11, I've chosen a gift from Starbucks that includes coffee, a mug, biscuits, and sweets.

SHORTCUT

For a list of merchants available on the Shopping channel, click Search & Explore in the Shopping channel window. You can also search for a particular kind of product, such as chocolates or diamonds.

Figure 12.11 Just the thing for the ultimate coffee break.

When you find a product in the Shopping channel, you'll be presented with a window such as the one in Figure 12.11. There will be a picture of the item along with a description and the price. At the bottom of the window is a button for ordering. When you order something, it goes into a virtual shopping cart. You can fill up the cart with many items from multiple merchants, so that when you're done, it will look like Figure 12.12. When you're ready to check out, you have to fill out your credit card and shipping information only once.

A Few Facts about Online Shopping

Most of the merchants available in the Shopping channel have their own areas on AOL. There are also links to merchants on the World Wide Web—you'll recognize them because they appear in a Web-type window. Either way, there's almost no risk involved in buying something, because online security is now almost impossible to defeat. Giving your credit card number online is no more dangerous than giving it to someone over the telephone, and it's a lot less risky than giving it to a waiter at a restaurant.

If you have any concerns about the safety of shopping on AOL, rest assured. AOL guarantees the security of all transactions with AOL-certified merchants and will protect you from liability in the unlikely event of credit card fraud. For details, use the keyword guarantee.

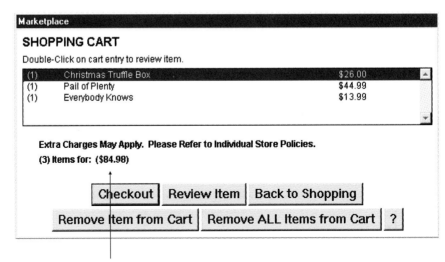

Here is the total price of everything in your shopping cart.

Figure 12.12 A shopping cart full of goodies

CAUTION

Online shopping doesn't necessarily offer you the best deals. Even if the price looks right, you should factor in shipping charges, which can make an item more expensive than if you just bought it in a store. But think of the convenience of doing all of your shopping from home!

That's it. The book's done. At this point, you may not be an expert, but you should have a good working knowledge with which to enjoy the myriad features and vast resources of the world's largest online service. Good luck, and if ever need assistance, remember the most important keyword of all: **help**.

Index